"The King's Kid"

By Karen "Lady Kay" Hilton-Sanders

This book is dedicated to

My Grandson Jasiah,

Grandson Omari that's resting easy in Heaven,

And

My Godchildren Layla and Jamir

Written by Karen "Lady Kay" Hilton-Sanders
Illustrated by R Van Hermawan

ISBN 9781686599255

I AM the King’s Kid

I AM the King's Kid
I have; I AM; and I will forever be

All that The King has created me to be

I AM
Unique in every way

I AM
grateful for The Kings Blessings that fill my day

The King watches over me
Both day and night

He is a lamp unto my feet

The King is my guiding light.

I AM never alone
Because the King is always near.

The King is my protector
So, I have nothing to fear.

The King guides my steps
Throughout my day.

And with HIS guidance
I know exactly what to say.

I AM the King's Kid

I was born to win

And I am never ever alone
Because the King lives within

And when it’s time for me to rest
I just lay down my head

And while I dream the King watches over me
While I AM asleep in my bed.

I AM ______________________________

and I Am the King's Kid

King's Kid Pledge

I, ___________________________ am The King's Kid

I love God and I Love others

And I love myself too

I honor and obey my parents

I won't steal or lie

I won't hurt others or myself

I will live by what the Bible says

I will forever be The King's Kid

King's Kid Prayer

Before I lay down I just want to say
Thank you Lord for the beautiful day
Thank you for being my side
Thank you for your love
Thanks for watching over me from above
I made it this day because of you
Thank you for my mother, father and all of my family
Thank you for all of your help
Thank you for sweet dreams and good sleep
Thank you for always being here with me
In Jesus name Amen

"You were created by God to be someone special. Someone who would change the world and make it a better place for everyone."

- You are amazing
- You are powerful
- You are wonderful
- You are the KING'S Kid

Karen "Lady Kay" Hilton- Sanders

Made in the USA
Monee, IL
24 November 2019

17363312R00017

Southwest by Two-Stroke

Riding Yamaha 350s to California

Brian Franzen, Mike Newlun and Jeffrey Ross

Afterword by
Doyle Ross

Published by Rogue Phoenix Press, LLP

ISBN: 978-1-62420-475-3

Credits
Cover Artist: Designs by Ms G

Team Black Rock and their friend Judy in Vacaville California June 1973

Dedication

To Those Who Have Ridden with Us

Preface

"Congratulations. You are now the owner of a new Yamaha R5C. The R5C is a high-performance motorcycle manufactured by the leading manufacturer of motorcycles in Japan.

The R5C, the newest and top of the Yamaha line, is designed for competition and high-speed road use. It features a rugged, powerful two-stroke twin cylinder engine and Autolube, the revolutionary lubricating system developed by the Yamaha Technical Research Laboratory and proven in all Yamaha models.

This manual explains some of the steps necessary for the operation and care of your new motorcycle. Please read it carefully to become thoroughly familiar with all the features and advantages built into your R5C" (1972 *R5C Owner's Manual*, courtesy Yamaha Motor Co., LTD, pub 278 28199-11).

“Two Lane Highway”

By Pure Prairie League (1975)

Soon it will be time to go
I don't want to leave, I guess you know
Maybe something new will come up
And I can come home for just a few more days
Get off this two lane highway
Is going my way, moving fast
Two lane highway
Is taking me home, home at last
You don't want me sleeping in
You turn around, I'm back again
I guess this time I'm really gone
But it don't seem right, I've been up all night
On this two lane highway
Is going my way, moving fast
Two lane highway
Is taking me home, home at last
Two lane highway
Is going my way, moving fast
Two lane highway
Is taking me home, home at last
Two lane highway
Going my way, moving fast
Two lane highway
Taking me home, home at last
Is taking me home, home at last
Oh, is taking me home, home at last
(Perhaps the best song EVER!)

I

Prelude

II

Background to 1973 Ride

III

Let’s Ride!

IV

Afterword by Doyle Ross

V

Thoughts in 2019

VI

Later Rides

I

Prelude

Prelude—Jeff

Three of us took a long motorcycle trip during early summer in 1973. Brian Franzen and I both had 1972 orange and black Yamaha 350 R5Cs. They were standard except for a luggage rack or small bar behind the seat. Brian had fabricated some highway pegs for cruising comfort. Mike Newlun was set to roll on a purple and white "chopped" 1970 R5 350. The bike had ten-inch fork extensions, Z handlebars, and a cool sissy bar.

A 1972 R5C in standard form.

Mike and his chopped 1970 R5A in Woodland Hills, California.

In the summer of 1973, I had just finished my freshman year at York College, and I was living at home. Brian had attended Nebraska Technical College in Milford the past six months, and he was working that summer for a bee keeper, Roger Bailey, out of McCool Junction, Nebraska. Mike was located down in Beatrice, living with our friend Dennis Osborne on 4th Street (Mike lives on 4th Street to this day.)

We left on our trip on June 15, 1973 and returned to Nebraska July 4th weekend. Or at least Brian and I did. Mike came back on July 2nd, but that's another story to be told later. Several bizarre incidents happened that spring which could have caused us to cancel or at least delay the trip. As I indicated earlier, I was attending college, worked a little bit for Roger Bailey the bee keeper, and I also worked as a carry-out at the Grand Central Super Value Grocery Store.

Sometime in late March or early April, at night, I was riding my Yamaha 350 home from the grocery story about 9:15 pm. I rounded the curve on Highway 81 as it wandered north through downtown York, dipped down to go through the underpass, and then slammed on the brakes and dumped my cycle to avoid hitting a car that was stopped in the roadway. To this day, I do not know why the AMC Gremlin was stopped at the bottom of the underpass.

The result is that I broke several small bones in my left foot. I wore a cast for about six weeks and hobbled on crutches around school till the semester concluded. Some of the female students felt sorry for me and carried my books occasionally. The professors probably thought I was out of my mind for riding a motorcycle. Mike has a memory of one of my crutches going out the window of his 1967 orange fastback Mustang as he was making a left turn. He says I laughed like crazy.

It never occurred to me to postpone or cancel the trip.

The damage to my motorcycle was minimal: a broken turn signal cover, a bent clutch lever, and a slightly-bent metal foot peg stub. (The foot peg contacted the pavement after breaking my foot!). That bike damage was all easily repaired by my good friends Jerry and Charlie at iconic Hurlbut's Cycle north of York. But I had to shift with my heel, rather than with the top of my foot like normal, for a while, once I got back on my machine. The foot was tender for most of the trip. Perhaps I was a little slower, a little more cautious. Maybe not. Seems like I pushed to get the cast removed a little early, so I could go on the bee work trip in late May before our motorcycle ride....

Jeff's R5 parked in the driveway of his York, Nebraska home.

Prelude—Mike

That summer of '73 was transitional for me. I had quit college. My school, Kearney State, was a teacher's college at the time. But I didn't want to be an educator. I didn't have a clear vision of my goals. I had enrolled in a Criminal Justice class with juniors and seniors and was asking myself, "What am I doing here?" That was the end of my college career.

Regarding our cross-country trip, I'm sure my family was worried about me. My grandfather told me they purchased an insurance policy on me to bury me in case I was killed during the trip.

I bought the Yamaha a few weeks before we left. I bought the bike from Ron Sawtell. He lived only a few blocks from Jeff in York, Nebraska. The night I got it, sometime in April 1973, there had been rain throughout the area. I borrowed some white coveralls from Jeff's dad. Then, I rode the motorcycle back to Beatrice in a light drizzle. The trip was eventful.

Doyle Ross in his ham shack wearing those famous white coveralls in 1958.

When entering the intersection in Dorchester on Highway 6, a driver or rider had to come to stop and turn right. There was a gap in the pavement from one surface to another. Since it was raining and there was a big puddle of water, I couldn't see the bottom of the gap. As I went to make the turn, I discovered the water was deeper than anticipated. Suddenly, the Yamaha slipped out from under me. I managed to place myself under the bike to protect it. I was lying in the puddle, thoroughly soaked, but the bike remained unscathed. I was okay but very cold and wet, so I gathered the bike up and limped into town to see a friend and to dry off and warm up. He wasn't home, so I borrowed his truck to go on to Beatrice. Turned out he was already in Beatrice. I told him what happened, and we returned his truck, and I rode my R5 home, all early the next morning.

Soon after, on a suggestion from Jeff, with only the tools under the seat, I pulled the cylinder heads, cylinders, and pistons, and took them down to the Yamaha dealer, Hurlbut's Cycle. I asked Charlie Hurlbut to bore them .010 over and to install new pistons and rings. When I inquired how long the process would take, Charlie said, "Just a minute." When he returned to the counter, he had a set of cylinders and matching rings. He said, “These have been done for another customer for a long time. Maybe by the time I get yours done, he will have the money to pay me.” So, I put the Yamaha back together. It ran great immediately.

Next, I took my ride to Jericho Cycles in Lincoln, Nebraska. There, I had ten-inch longer fork tubes and Z bars installed. That kind of sharp-point handlebar could gut you, but I didn't worry about such things. When I got the R5 back, the mechanic said, “You have ruined a good bike.” Nice. He sent along a new brake cable, but I didn't have the right hardware to hook up the cable to the drum brake. Pretending to be a mechanical engineer, I used a coat hanger to finish the linkage. (It never let me down, but I sure thought about the brakes heading down through the mountain passes later in Arizona!) Anyway, we left for California one week after I chopped the Yamaha.

Prelude—Brian

How did we ever come up with “Team Black Rock” as a name? We joked about that term most of the late winter and spring of '73. But the name stuck. I had our shirts made at a t-shirt shop in Lincoln. They cost about twelve dollars apiece. None of us saw the movie until much later in life, but that phrase, “A bad day at Black Rock”—well, we seemed to use it quite a bit that spring as we prepared for the big bike trip. Sort of a linguistic gem of the seventies, perhaps.

Something happened to me in April of ‘73 that might have affected the trip. One afternoon, for some reason, I let Judy, the girl from York College I was dating, “drive” my Yamaha. I was seated behind her, showing her how to work the throttle and clutch and brakes. And hanging on.

Well, somewhere near York College, we were making a right turn when she accelerated too hard, taking us wide, and hit the front of a car parked on the north side of 12th Street. The impact, plus me sitting behind her, pushed her over the handlebars. The wreck resulted in her going to the ER to get checked out. She had big bruises on her thighs and lots of soreness, but nothing was broken.

My Yamaha’s front fork tubes were bent back into the engine, and the bike was completely out of commission. Our crash happened about three or four blocks from my house. At home, my dad had a plywood dolly with little wheels that I procured, and I eventually carried it back to the accident scene. Then I loaded up the machine and rolled it back those three or four blocks to our house. Not long after, Hurlbut's Cycle Shop replaced the bent tubes with new ones and I was once again good to go. I was so concerned about that Yamaha—and visiting Judy in the hospital. Of course, later, on the trip, I would see her again.

Bee work in North Dakota Just Before Motorcycle Trip—Jeff

Brian and I were both employees of the Blue Valley Apiary back in the early seventies. I was essentially a weekend or seasonal worker—Brian had a longer, more significant stint with the bee business owned by Mr. Roger Bailey of McCool Junction, Nebraska. We did all kinds of work, from honey collection in the fall to hive body and super (the boxes stacked on hives containing the honeycomb frames) construction and feeding the bees in the winter time. I remember being stunned, overjoyed almost, when Roger raised my wage from $2.00 to $2.50 an hour in the spring of 1973.

Roger ran about 10,000 hives in Nebraska. As his operation expanded, he would move about 5000 hives down to the Nacogdoches and Alvin, Texas area in the winter time. He had a Peterbilt tractor–two trailer rig especially dedicated for moving the bees back and forth. The hive bodies and supers would be placed on the two trailers behind the Peterbilt truck sitting on pallets and moved by a Bobcat forklift. Large nets were placed over the hives to keep the bees from drifting or escaping.

Well, in late May-early June of '73, Roger decided he was going to transport a few hundred hives up to the Dickinson, North Dakota area to take advantage of the sweet clover and alfalfa fields. So, many bees made a very long trip from Texas to North Dakota. Dave, Roger's truck driver, brought the bees up to Dickinson a week or so before we arrived.

Brian and I drove a straight truck with a trailer carrying our bee suits, smokers, hive tools, and hive supers to North Dakota. Our mission was to set up the bees in predetermined ranchers' fields. (Roger was always busy planning with farmers and ranchers for places to put his bees. As you know, bees and plants have a "symbiotic" relationship.) We spent over a week driving around the countryside, grooving to "Radar Love," working with various folks, and thriving in a motel room after work.

That was hard work. We had maps and scribbled notes, but we didn't always know exactly where we were going. Some of the pastures and ditches were rough. The hives had all been offloaded from the Peterbilt trailers in a field outside of Glen Ulin—and Brian and I would take pallets of bees out to sites and super-up the hives. Of course, we wore bee suits and used the smokers to calm the bees. This was generally effective, but those bees were not happy after being netted and jostled about for a thousand miles or so.

One windy afternoon, I was stung several times in the face. My veil kept blowing up against my cheeks, and the bees we were unloading, probably angry after that three-day road trip from Texas, took their frustration out on me. I had to take a day off. I looked a lot like Mr. Potato Head. After that week, I spent more time working in the plant doing maintenance and construction and less time working out in the yards. Well, anyway, I recovered from the stinging beat-down in time to make our motorcycle trip westward.

We were anxious to get back to Nebraska and prep for our Pacific ride. As the schedule turned out, we had very little turnaround time between driving the straight truck and equipment back to Nebraska and getting ready to ride out. Our energy level was amazing. I think in many ways that trip to North Dakota really toughened me and helped mature me.

Bee Business—Brian

We had good, state-of-the-art equipment to work with. The Peterbilt was a cab-over tractor Roger bought brand new from a dealer in Grand Island. That Peterbilt pulled tandem twenty-foot flatbed trailers, so it was easier to pull, one at a time, into farmers' pastures. Jeff and I traveled in and worked from a new Chevy twenty-four-foot straight truck with a flat bed pulling a twenty-foot trailer.

Roger, an innovator, a leader, a pioneer adapter in the independent apiary industry at the time, was strategically increasing his business model by going into new geographies.

The Bobcat forklift was a new technology for bee keepers in the early seventies, putting equipment in the fileld. Interestingly, we dipped supers in wax, rather than painting them, to withstand the weather. That was a cutting-edge idea at the time also.

The bee keeper/Peterbilt semi driver's name was Dave. For what it's worth, Dave was a Seventh-Day Adventist and would never work Saturdays. But he would work Sundays. Since I didn't want to vegetate in a hotel room in Alvin, Texas for two days, I would sit for Saturday and work Sunday with Dave. He was a quiet, hardworking guy, not dissimilar from Roger Bailey, just with a different cadence.

We wintered bees in Nacogdoches and Alvin, Texas. I believe Roger met Woody, a bee keeper from Dickinson who introduced the idea of branching into North Dakota, in Alvin. They worked out a deal where Roger set up the Dakotan around Alvin, and then Woody would reciprocate and help Roger find locations in western North Dakota.

I made three trips to North Dakota that '73 summer. The first was with Roger. I finished my first two quarters of school at Milford, and as soon as I was done, I went with Roger to Dickinson. Milford must have ended in early May.

Roger had been helping Dave load bees in Alvin, and then he headed back up to McCool Jct. where we convened before heading to North Dakota.

Dave drove the semi-truck by himself with the actual beehives (hive bodies). Roger and I chained his pickup onto the bed of the Chevy straight truck and towed the Bobcat behind on its trailer. (Unfortunately, I ran a chain over the axle of his pickup and crushed a brake line. Roger had to get the line repaired at the Ford dealership in Dickinson). We met up with Dave, who brought up the semi load of bees in their hive boxes from south Texas.

I worked with Dave to unload the hives onto the ground in a rancher's field between Hebron and Glen Ullin. Roger and Woody, the local bee keeper, flew around in Woody's private airplane to view the area topography and spot future bee sites.

Leaning out of the Chevy truck with the Peterbilt truck, Dave, and bee hives near Glen Ullin, North Dakota

Bee keepers (the ones I knew of anyway) were all small-plane pilots. That way, they could fly and scout locations quickly from the air and mark them on a rural topo map. As I mentioned earlier, Woody and Roger flew around with a topo map and made **X's** on the map where they found a suitable location with sweet clover and alfalfa. Then later, Roger would contact the owner or the rancher and get permission to put bees on the site (and get special instructions about access to gates and such).

He would typically drive out to the ranch and meet the owner and talk business. Then Roger and Woody would hammer a four-foot length of lathe into the ground with a flag-like piece of fluorescent banner. So, Jeff and I later had visual and written instructions about where to set up the bee yards. Roger and I returned home in a few days, and on the way back he told me, "You and Jeff can take supers up there to North Dakota and set up those hives."

On my second trip, Jeff and I departed York late May for North Dakota. Our mission was to set up the hives with supers (the boxes for the bees to store honey) in those various predetermined, flagged locations in the area east of Dickinson, North Dakota.

Loaded straight truck and trailer with supers at Brian's parents' home in York, NE.

I took along the new Eagles album (*Desperado*) on a cassette, but there was too much noise inside the truck cab to enjoy the music.

We took Highway 281 north from Grand Island, up to O'Neill, and then across the Fort Randall Dam, into South Dakota. We finally got to Jamestown, North Dakota and headed west on I-94. Heavy wind was blowing from the north as we drove west of Bismarck. Our straight truck had a four-speed transmission with a split axle. I had to drive in third gear, split-axle-high, just to maintain enough RPMs to move along at, maybe, fifty mph. We discovered a Canadian AM radio station from Manitoba that provided us with good rock music most of the trip including, "Waterloo" and "Radar Love."

Brian driving Chevy straight truck.

At some point, we took the truck into the Dickinson Chevy dealership (under warranty) to get the torsion-bar-suspension driver's seat fixed. After that, it felt so much better riding higher and having the torsion bar system work correctly.

After settling in to our routine and learning the ropes, the two of us would talk every evening with Woody to get the updated map for the next day's locations and specific, useful, deployment information.

Jeff and I would go out and find those stakes with the fluorescent banners based on a topographic map and instructions, sometimes driving fifty miles or more on graveled roads. We would set up the bee yards and then move on to the next site, typically setting up five or six a day. We repeated the process for several days, driving each morning from our base in Dickinson to sites around Glen Ullin and Hebron and then returning in the late afternoon.

Brian Franzen, Bee worker

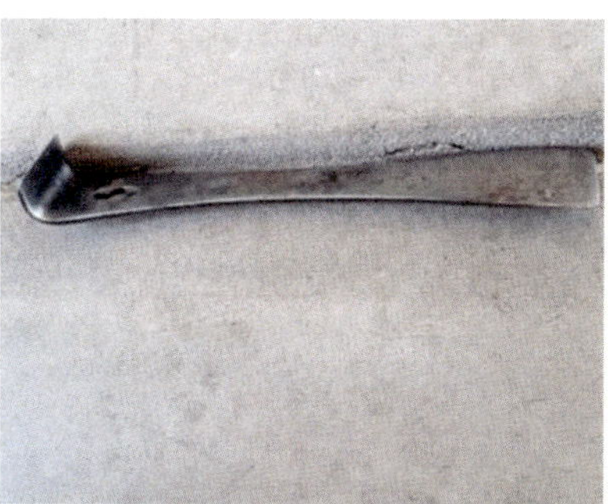

Brian's Hive Tool

Jeff in a North Dakota pasture, holding his hive tool.

Big-sky country dominates the landscape in western North Dakota. Sometimes I would gain speed in the straight truck and we would try to "catch a little air" as we crested a hill while hurrying to the next bee yard. Once, after leaping through the air as we crested the hill, we drove right into a "T" intersection. Wow! No time to slow down! That could have been trouble if I drove through a barbed wire fence. But thankfully, we passed through the intersection, unscathed, into a level field. There was no fence or tractor or car to hit. Just prairie. We dodged trouble.

We headquartered in Dickinson at the same motel where Roger and I had stayed previously. Jeff and I became friends with two young ladies who worked there. One was the manager and the other was the housekeeper. We went with them to a "woodsy" or two. These were parties out in the country with a bonfire and beer. Great times and part of North Dakota culture I will never forget.

Once, while working on hive bodies back at the plant in McCool Jct., I shot a staple through my thumb nail during a life-lesson episode. Nothing innovative about that!

I've concluded that Roger Bailey had a major impact on my life. He trusted an 18-year-old to drive a big truck and trailer thousands of miles by himself (and his side-kick!) and set up his bee operation in North Dakota. Our Dickinson-area bee experience gave me the courage and boldness to tackle a three-thousand-mile motorcycle trip on a 350 Yamaha. Yes, working for Roger Bailey gave me confidence to do things like the big ride to the west coast. He didn't think twice about giving me the keys to the truck. What could go wrong?

The Yamaha R5—Jeff

I sense it is difficult to separate the geographical and spiritual nature of our trip from the mechanical aspects of the motorcycles. Two-stroke twins and triples pretty much ruled the streets in the late sixties and early seventies, at least for younger guys. The howl of air intakes, the "ring-a-ding" clatter of a decelerating two-stroke, and the glorious clouds of dense blue exhaust smoke visible at most intersections, well, that was all part of the deal. They made plenty of useable power, accelerated briskly, and required little maintenance. Harleys seemed large, slow, overpriced, and unreliable to us. Our Yamahas were fun and fast!

My R5 could not stay with a Triumph Bonneville 650, but it was far faster than Triumph 500s and the ubiquitous Honda CB 350s of the time.

I have an extensive two-stroke background. I learned to ride on my dad's 1968 Kawasaki Avenger A7SS 350 (red with chrome tank panels) on the dirt road behind the Rancho Del Sol Trailer park in Casa Grande, Arizona, where we lived back in 1969 (until the summer of 1971 when we moved to Nebraska). When I turned 16 in 1970, dad bought me a new black and white 1969 Yamaha YR2C 350. (Man, I wish I had that bike now.)

Yamaha YR2C

I rode it for about a year, and then we traded it in on a bright yellow and white, new 1970 Kawasaki Avenger 350 A7SS of my own. The rotary valve induction Kawasaki two-stroke 350 was good for an honest 110 mph.

They wheelied easily but didn't handle so well.

During my senior year of high school, in York, Nebraska, I rode a 1971 Kawasaki 500 Mach III—another book could be written about my exploits on that space-age Blue 500. For now, let me say it was terrifyingly fast, had a slight high-speed wobble, and developed some unsettling clutch bearing noise that led me back to Yamahas and the R5C.

The motorcycle magazines of the time loved the R5C. *Cycle,* in a comparison of several 350s, called it "the thinking man's superbike." However, after riding a 60 bhp 500 Kawasaki for a year (0-60 mph in four seconds, 12.9 second ¼ miles), I was never that impressed with the R5's performance. But it was a good, solid motorcycle which handled like a dream and looked very modern. I had loved my 1969 YR2C so much, and this 1972 descendant was a very polished, sophisticated street bike. The 21-cubic inch engine made about 36 bhp, went about 100 mph flat out, and managed around forty mpg. I knew Yamahas were dependable, and the R5 just looked right for the early 1970s.

Here is some basic info about the Yamaha. The R5 was produced between 1970 and 1972. They moved along on 18-inch spoked wheels with a Dunlop 3.25-inch tube-type ribbed tire up front and a Dunlop 3.50-inch tube type K70 on the back. Tires lasted maybe 4000 miles, so I am sure we were all close to needing new rubber when we returned from our long ride to the coast. The R5 had drum brakes front and rear which worked okay, a steering damper, a separate tach and speedo, and a refined version of the company's Autolube automatic oil injection system.

Two-strokes (like outboards and chain saws) burn oil in their gasoline to lubricate engine bearings and pistons (hence the noise and smell). In the old days, oil had to be mixed manually. A prescribed amount would be poured into the gas tank each time a two-stroke bike was fueled. But with modern systems like Autolube, oil is added to a separate tank and then automatically metered into the carburetors for lubrication. I probably had to add a quart of oil to the Autolube tank about every four hundred miles or so.

People constantly debated the kind of oil to use in those systems. I knew some guys who just used any old 30W automotive oil. I typically used Yamaha two-stroke oil specifically designed for air-cooled motorcycles, though there was a time or two when I had to use outboard oil. But let me point out directly: in at least 100K miles of two-stroke riding between 1968 and 1981, I never suffered any debilitating mechanical failure.

I generally used automotive Automatic Transmission Fluid (ATF) in the five-speed gearbox. That was changed infrequently. I never did have a clutch or transmission problem on any of my bikes, but Brian did have an issue as described later.

Those R5s had carburetors, not fuel injection. We rarely had to fiddle with air/fuel mixtures, needle clips, or idle screws. Those bikes just ran and ran and ran.

The Yamahas used chain final drive, and the chain required constant attention. I adjusted the chain (tightened it) every couple hundred miles, and we carried cans of chain oil along with us always. Any rain storm would motivate me to oil the chain more often, but typically I would oil the chain every other gas stop (two hundred miles or so). Chain oil was (is!) messy. The bike's rear wheel, mufflers, and tire were frequently splattered by excess oil. (And so was my jacket or shirt.) Twenty-first century chain oil sticks better, much better, but it can still be messy.

Ignition chores were handled by points and condenser. Timing was easy to set with a TDC (Top Dead Center) dial and a feeler gauge. Spark plugs occasionally fouled, but we honestly didn't have any significant issues on our trip. I believe I checked my timing in Tempe, Arizona, while we were briefly visiting my aunt and uncle, Steve and Deanna Cooley. By the way, no points adjustment was required.

However, at my aunt and uncle's, I got all oily and greasy replacing a drive chain. This is a lesson for anyone replacing a chain. I had picked up a new chain at Apache Cycles when Brian procured a new countershaft sprocket. After having lunch with Steve and Deanna, I went out to their carport (in the shade) to put on the new chain. The OEM chain just wore out, I guess, because it had several tight spots and was becoming very noisy. I first noticed the problem in Albuquerque but thought I would wait till we got to Phoenix to make the repair.

Replacing a motorcycle chain is normally not complicated or messy, especially on the old kind that used a master link. For whatever reason (might have been the heat), I took the old one completely off before attaching the new chain to the old chain with the master link. I could have just rolled the new chain on to the sprockets by pulling on the old chain. But no—too easy. I got greasy and messy trying to stick that new chain onto the countershaft sprocket by hand.

One interesting characteristic of all two-stroke motorcycles is that they have no engine braking ability. Unlike with a four-stroke engine, rolling off the throttle on a two-stroke motorcycle doesn't help the bike slow down all that much. The engine doesn't provide significant back pressure or braking, so you just roll along. Eventually, the front drum brake on the R5 series was replaced by a disk brake on the 1973 and later RD series. But the drum brakes were capable enough on the R5 to haul it down from speed.

As touring machines, our R5s were adequate. They rolled along at seventy mph (indicated) feeling very under stressed. The tach showed a red line of 8500 rpm, and at sixty-five mph, the motor was only turning about 5000 rpm.

But they were rather primitive. Instrumentation was minimal, and the seat was barely comfortable. We just piled bags and sleeping gear up against a sissy bar or short luggage rack bar and rode off. Sound systems or GPS? Come on, man. We carried old-time paper maps and notes and never got lost. I tried listening to an AM//FM radio using small ear phones (primitive ear buds of the time) but was unsuccessful. AM was drowned out by static noise from the spark plugs firing, and FM was drowned out by the howl of the engine and wind.

Later I owned a Yamaha RD 250, a Kawasaki KH400 triple, an RD 350, a Yamaha RD 400, and a Suzuki Le Mans 750 "water buffalo." All great bikes I should have kept!

I currently own a 1973 CS3 Yamaha 200 twin "café racer."

One last point. Back in the 1970s, 350 cc motorcycles were marketed as middle-weight machines suitable for many tasks. Nowadays, motorcycles in that engine displacement class are viewed as quickly-outgrown beginner bikes barely suited for highway or freeway travel. Times change.

My Two-Stroke History—Mike

Probably when I was around ten, my dad owned a Skelly gas station in Aurora, Nebraska where we lived. He picked up Bridgestone motorcycles to sell. I remember we had a red 175cc road bike and a black 250 cc also. He was a man always looking for adventure.

One Sunday, he and I rode the black 250cc, and his partner and his son rode the 175cc bike, to an archery tournament in nearby Hastings. This was about an hour ride each way. We had our bows in boxes, with our arrows and quivers stuffed inside, bungeed crossways on the back of the bikes. We wore all white as was the custom of the day. We had great fun. And on the way back, I got to ride up front and take the controls. I was in heaven. Riding on the Bridgestone was the fastest and furthest I had ever gone on a motorcycle!

Later, when I was about thirteen or fourteen, Dad picked up a nice little red Kawasaki. I don't recollect the engine size, but I do remember the bike had what looked like a snow tire on the back. And yes, I did ride it in the snow. I rode it for hours around the gas pumps in first and second gear—sometimes with the baffle out. That is until I was given the ultimatum: "Put it back in or put the bike away."

Mike riding in the snow 1969

I rode it till my hands and feet were numb and had to be thawed out painfully. But I never lost my desire to ride. I would find bikes for sale and beg for permission to buy them, but it was never given.

Even so, one time a Kawasaki 238 cc Sidewinder dirt bike followed me home when I was a high school senior. I had to keep that rig. That 238 ran strong until it seized doing sixty mph right alongside Jeff riding his Mach III 500cc. Riding that Mach III after tooling along on that 238 was like getting out of a Willys Jeep and getting in a Dodge Charger. So smooth, and holy s**t, that triple was fast. I was surprised he traded it in for an R5, but they really had different purposes. I still can't believe he traded, though. He has a "thing" for smaller-displacement motorcycles.

Jeff and his blue Mach III in Oklahoma, 1972. Photo taken by his dad, Doyle Ross, who was riding the green Honda CB 450.

My Two-Stroke History: The AT-1 Yamaha Enduro—Brian

A Yamaha AT-1 Enduro

In the spring of 1971, my dad went out with me to Hurlbut's Cycle Shop north of York, Nebraska, to look at motorcycles. I thought he meant really "just to look," but Dad suddenly said, "Do you want to get one?" I ended up buying a new, red, 1971 Yamaha AT1C Enduro motorcycle, and a sparkly red ¾ helmet with a flat face shield, for cash, with my own money! I was surprised. I rode it home that day and thought I was the (most scared) king of the world!

My first memory of owning the motorcycle was going home from high school for lunch. The school lunch period was long enough, and we lived close enough to school, for me to ride home and eat lunch. I came out of the parking lot north of the building, turned right, and accelerated (to impress anyone watching), when one of my classmates backed out of a parking spot along the street.

Being new at riding the machine, I didn't have muscle-memory entrenched yet. Before I could pull in the clutch and brake enough, I grazed the right side of her car with my left handlebar. I was so embarrassed. After talking with her and looking at the side of her car (ignoring the bent clutch handle on my bike), we agreed there wasn't any damage to report to insurance or to the police, and we went our separate ways.

Of course, when I got home, I didn't say a word to my mom (and washed off the small cut on my left hand). Certainly, one of the first of many riding life-lessons.

I learned to ride off-road on trails, on sand (at the abandoned sand pit east of York), and by racing (on the dirt "track" across the creek by Hurlbut's Cycle Shop). I got pretty good at doing extended wheelies with that AT-1. I would accelerate into second gear, drop off the gas and stay in gear, then immediately go full-on throttle to get the front end up. I would moderate the gas to keep the wheelie going.

Several of us around York owned Enduros, and we would ride and race off-road as a group. Even though they had 250s or, in one case, a 360, we all rode together and raced each other. One day, after a fun time of hill-climbing at the sand pit, we went into the famous Sackschewsky Bar in Waco. A few of the older riders had a beer, while we under-age guys just had soda or water.

Then we finished the day up at the dirt track by Hurlbut's Cycle and engaged in some racing. They would always give me a head start because I rode the smallest cc engine. I would ride like crazy to stay in front of them. At this primitive track, I learned corners are pretty good equalizers to larger cc bikes.

I learned another riding life-lesson: don't drink alcohol and ride. As we were racing that day, the owner of the 360 Yamaha passed me coming out of a corner, and I watched him honking along in front of me. He came up on the next corner and the rear tire started sliding out, then caught, and the bike tossed him off over the right side. We all stopped to help him get back up. He was holding his arm. I later learned he landed on his right shoulder, tearing it up pretty good, and the next week, his wife made him sell the motorcycle. He ran a heating and air conditioning service and needed his arms to perform his work. He couldn't fully function until he healed up. Don't drink and then ride!

I customized that 125 some. I installed a higher front fender, bought an expansion chamber exhaust pipe, and added a compression-release valve for the cylinder. The compression-release was a valuable device to use while racing with friends. You could go into a corner faster, hit the compression-release valve to let the engine help slow you down without locking up the rear tire, then quickly down shift coming out of the corner, release the valve, and "gas it." I think it made me way faster! One of the mechanics at Hurlbut's told me a racing truism that my experience with the compression-release valve illustrated: The faster you come out of a corner, the faster you must enter the corner.

The expansion chamber exhaust was pretty cool, I thought. It made the bike louder and (the catalog said) made me faster. Of course, the chamber was a wide-open and unmuffled exhaust and was completely illegal to run on the street. I was too cheap to purchase a commercial muffler for the expansion pipe. So, I made one of my own, a pop can filled with steel wool held on with springs, to ride in town. That home-made muffler unfortunately reduced the performance of the bike, so I didn't keep the pipe for too long. I remember going home fairly late one night with the expansion pipe and muffler on. Before starting out, I removed the muffler (while it was cool to the touch), bungeed it onto the luggage rack, and blasted back home, riding fast and loud! A half-block from home, I down-shifted to neutral and shut the engine off and coasted in so my folks wouldn't hear me.

I rode that 125 *all the time,* in all weather, because it was my transportation. I recall I got a job at the York Super Value Grocery store and rode the bike home from work one winter evening in the snow, with my feet out like outriggers. I was so proud of myself for not dropping the bike once!

In early summer of 1971, the federal government was tearing down the surplus grain storage bin at Bradshaw, Nebraska. It was the best paying job I ever had at that time, paying six dollars an hour. I rode the 125 over there to work. One day, I realized the oil in the auto-oiler tank was low, but I had to get to work and gambled that I could get there before the oil ran out. I lost the bet, and the engine seized up on me on the way over to Bradshaw. I kept going since I had to get to work. I reasoned that I would buy a quart of oil at the local gas station for the ride home, then get the cylinder bored out and install a new piston and rings, which I did later.

I traded my AT-1 Enduro for a new 350cc R5C during my senior year in high school. I was also driving a white, four-door,1964 Rambler at that time, so I split time more from the motorcycle riding.

One warm February weekend day in 1972, after getting my R5C 350, Jeff and I had a nice ride. We took our bikes south from York on Highway 81 to Fairmont and turned west on Highway 6 and then north to Aurora, Nebraska on Highway 14. We stopped at his grandparents' house around four pm to rest up and get a bite to eat.

By the time we headed back, it was after dark and getting colder. We rode for a few miles, becoming increasingly chilled, while we moved along at highway speed. Eventually, we signaled each other to pull over. We talked it over, using the logic that cold is cold, so we should run the bikes up to eighty or ninety and get back home quicker. Without further discussion, we crouched low behind the handlebars and cranked it up and raced back to York, arriving thoroughly "frozen."

My Teen History with Cars—Mike

Something that makes me a little different than Brian and Jeff involves my teenage history with cars—cool cars. Dad was an excellent mechanic. Many cars came our way. My first car, when I was old enough to drive, was more likely my third or fourth car.

The first two were 1960 Ford Galaxies, if I remember correctly. The first and better car was a 4-door with a 352 automatic. The second was a 292 Y block with a 3-speed on the tree. It was a 2-door. Much cooler, but the motor wasn't nearly as good as the other. Both were pale green. They were not anything special. But they were supposed to be mine. I never fully liked either, so they were moved on.

Another car that came into my life was a '64 blue Corvair with a 4-speed stick. Dad had put new bearings in the motor, an easy repair for him. He could fix anything. I loved the car. Then, Ralph Nader entered the picture with his book, *Unsafe at Any Speed*, and suddenly that car wasn't for me. The Corvair was deemed a death trap, and we could do better.

As luck would have it, another car came into my life; a Red '64 Plymouth Sport Fury, with red bucket seats, a 383 V-8, a Hurst 4-speed, and mag wheels on the back. The Plymouth was a repossession at the car lot next to our gas station, and Dad did almost all their work. He thought the Fury would be a great first car for me. He took the car for a test drive and missed the highway when he left the station. Come to find out the Fury had been driven hard.

The previous owner broke the steering box off the frame, and there were two full turns of play in the steering. This issue was the first thing we fixed. I wasn't to get my permit for a couple of months yet, so it seemed time stood still. I washed it almost every day and I waxed it often, waiting and imagining cruising around the courthouse square in Aurora with the windows down.

The Fury turned out to be a great car and the first of many Mopars. I loved my Mopars. I still do. My undoing was the price of gas. The Fury burned high octane Ethyl and that was expensive compared to "regular" gas. I sold the Plymouth after a while when a 1955 Chevy Bel-Aire 2-door hard top showed up at the gas station.

What red-blooded American male didn't want one of those? But the Bel-Aire didn't have an engine or transmission. The car had been painted metallic dark green and put in a corn cob shed. It was once pretty, but goats had been allowed to walk all over it. I buffed the Chevy with a polisher for a week. When I was finished, it glowed. Dad and I put together a 327 and a 3-speed manual transmission coupled with a "Sparkomatic" shifter. (The shifter, despite the name, was junk.) I put chrome wheels and poly-glass tires on the Chevy, and it looked super.

One afternoon, Dad backed the Chevy out of the wash rack to put it on the lift to put the dual exhaust on. After he backed the car out and lined it up to the second door, he got this look on his face and started revving up the engine. He lit up the tires and, after putting on a show by leaving black marks on the pavement, he pulled the car in and looked at my friend Dennis and me and said, "Don't you ever do that!"

At sixteen, I wasn't allowed to leave town without permission. So, the first thing I did when I got my license was ask to Dad if I could visit my grandparents in York. Permission was received, and my buddy and I were off on an adventure. York was only twenty miles distant, but that was a long way in those days for a new driver. I didn't tell Dad the starter on the car was out. We just parked the car on a hill and gave the Chevy a shove when necessary.

The car was so attractive I couldn't go anywhere without someone wanting to buy it from me. After only four weeks, I gave up and sold the Bel Aire. Truthfully, I had my fill. I was tired of being approached to sell the car and was very glad to get my '64 Plymouth back. There was no comparison to the quality of the cars.

Then, one day, while pumping gas at the Sinclair station, I caught a glimpse of what I thought was a good-looking vehicle with potential: a white '58 Ford Fairlane. A few weeks passed, but I tracked the owner down and bought it for the hefty sum of $125. This Ford was a diamond in the rough. The Fairlane had started life as a six-cylinder automatic, but someone had hung a clutch pedal and installed a 292 Y block V8. The Ford had a 4 bbl. AFB carburetor and a 3-speed overdrive.

The motor smoked a bit, and the front seat needed some attention. Other than that, the interior was perfect. Well, almost. The steering wheel had to go. The thing was huge like all steering wheels of the fifties. Dad told me not to change the wheel, so I did. Thing was, I did a good job, and when I was done, I received his blessing. I fixed the seat. Then I pulled the motor and I put in a 312 Y block Thunderbird motor and put the 4 bbl. AFB carb on. Wow, what a difference! The body was perfect, except it sat too low.

I raised the front end. We cut the pads off the third member and refitted them on top. This allowed me to raise the car's stance and keep the same shocks and springs. I eliminated the stock single exhaust and brought a dual exhaust out the side of the car in front of the back wheels. The car looked and sounded amazing. I also bought the rear end out of a '60 Thunderbird, so I could use taller gears in the Fairlane. The new gears were perfect. It went from indicating 3500 rpm at seventy-five mph to showing 1700 rpm at sixty-five mph and 1900 at seventy-five mph. I don't know how fast the car could go, as I never ever got "there." But that Ford did get thirty-three miles per gallon.

After driving the Fairlane for about a year, another opportunity came along in the form of a Blue 1968 Dodge Charger. The owner had washed it every day. A very clean and modern car. He said he waxed it once a week and raced it on Sundays. The Charger had 77,000 miles on the odometer and rode and drove just like it came off the showroom floor. The Dodge became mine for $1100. This was the car that I went to college with and then sold to buy my Yamaha for the trip. Selling that car troubles me yet, but most all the cars that I bought and sold still haunt me. There is enough of a story about my cars for a book by itself.

Oh, and while I had the Charger, I also bought a '57 Ford 2-door station wagon with a custom paint job and nice interior. I had to put a motor in that one, too, so I found a 272 Y block coupled to an air-cooled automatic transmission. I had to sell the wagon because I wasn't allowed to insure two cars at a time. So, I sold the wagon and the money was used to pay for part of my college tuition. I sold that Ford for a whopping seven hundred dollars. That was a lot of money for such a car in those days.

By the way, we raced stock cars too. We were around a community of car people who knew engines and racing. Because of this, we sometimes found powerful exotic cars. I don't know the details, but Dad frequently found them. One very interesting car was a '62 Ford 2-door. That car was black on black with a 4-speed. This beast had bucket seats front and rear. The console went all the way to the back. Under the hood was, I think, a 426. The engine had a huge air cleaner that covered either 2 4bbl. carbs or a tri-power set-up. I was in awe. The motor needed rebuilding, but the body was solid and needed only a small repair. I don't know what ever happened to that car. If I would have been turned loose, the motor would have ended up in a '57 black Ford Custom 300. I always imagined that Ford as a gasser.

We raced a 1955 Buick Century. In our second year of competition, we worked out the bugs. That car was originally picked up by the Aurora Jaycees organization when they cleaned up junk around town. The Century was a former mail car, had 150,000 miles of service use, and then two years of racing. Our Buick never used any oil. The car was bone stock. And we were the points champion in our second season of racing. Almost everyone thought we were doing something illegal, but we weren't. We dared everyone to claim the motor, but no one else raced a Buick. Dad also built a '58 Ford Custom stock car, but that didn't work out so well.

I was a very lucky teenager. We had our own mini test track behind the gas station. From time to time, I got to take out the stock car and test or break-in a new motor.

As you can see, I was able to drive and work on many interesting automobiles before I turned 18! I love motorcycles, but I really love cars, too!

II

Background to 1973 Ride

Background to the 1973 Ride—Jeff

The extensive motorcycle ride would take us from Beatrice, Nebraska (where Mike was living at the time) through Kansas to Philmont Scout Ranch in New Mexico, Albuquerque, Phoenix, San Diego, LA, Vacaville, Lake Tahoe, Ely, Denver, and then back to Nebraska. We had relatives, friends, acquaintances, and girlfriends to see all along the journey. Some nights we camped out, some nights we stayed in a friend's tent or travel trailer, some nights we had regular showers and regular beds and access to a swimming pool.

In this text, we will share our memories about the trip and American culture at the time. You might think it odd that we used 21-cubic inch two-stroke motorcycles for a 3500-mile trip across the continent. We had no cell phones, roadside assistance insurance coverage, body armor, custom ear plugs, grip warmers, or sound systems.

We loved it. The early seventies were different than the sixties, but not that much different. The call of the open road, the draw of western skies and the Pacific Ocean—all very powerful. None of us were worried about breaking down or the costs of the trip. We had to go see western America. And we did.

Team Black Rock

Mike's extant Team Black Rock shirt

Brian's Team Black Rock shirt

We had white and yellow ¾ sleeve t-shirts made with our "club" name, "Team Black Rock." Apparently, our name was based on the 1955 thriller, *Bad Day at Black Rock*, starring Spencer Tracy and Robert Ryan (about a stranger who comes to a small town looking for a man and is met with disdain from nearly every local). But the other fellows might have a different sense of where we got our brand. Brian and Mike told me they both still have their shirts. Mine might be in a box somewhere, come to think of it. I don't let the past go easily.

Brian and Mike each wore a denim jacket. Mike's jacket had some cool rivets. Brian wore a ¾ coverage helmet with a seventies-era face shield. Mike had a full-coverage Grant helmet with some powder blue stars painted on the sides. I wore a black Naugahyde jacket and a white Bell full-coverage helmet. I used some cheap clip-on sun glasses. (Seems to me like we always were facing the sun and confronting a headwind.) Brian had an American flag visor he wore when we weren't on the motorcycles. He kept it under a bungee cord when riding, and he had a fishing bobber attached to a button hole on his jacket. Mike looked the most like a "biker" of the time, but we all had long hair and big ideas.

Mike's Jacket

Brian (with wife Karen on their honeymoon) and his Fishing Bobber Jacket (1976)

We occasionally rubbed on some Coppertone "sun tan lotion," and we might have stuck some cotton balls in our ears periodically to impede the howling noise of wind and two-stroke motors.

Luggage, Cooking, Camping, and Overnighters—Jeff

We travelled very lightly, and our gear was minimal. I had a thin grey sleeping bag and a canvas ground cloth but carried no pillow. I would wad up my jacket or a shirt or sweatshirt for a pillow. I had a bag stuffed with some clothes. Bungee cords were our friends. Much of the technology available now simply didn't exist. I'm sure somebody had a can of Sterno fuel and a pan tucked into an old canvas pack somewhere, but we didn't have the same interest in food or exotic camping gear that nineteen-year-olds relish today. We were three thin dudes who didn't need a lot of calories.

I have noticed in old few photos that Mike and I had canteens strapped on, or hanging on, to our bikes. There was no bottled water back then. I wonder how many canteen-carrying motorcycles roll down the highway in 2019?

We camped overnight a few times. Brian addresses that below, but we basically ate our meals at truck stops, or "ma and pa" restaurants along the two-lane highways. Team Black Rock typically relied on the generosity of the folks we stayed with or visited along the 3500-mile circuit.

Sissy Bar—Brian

I mounted a sissy bar on the back of the bike. I tied my back pack with all my personal stuff to the bar. I used two short black rubber bungees in an X- pattern across the back of sissy bar and the pack. It kept the load stable. I put my sleeping bag on the front of the pack, so I could lean back on it and then put my feet up on the pegs I added to the frame in front by the engine. For the bar, I just used a piece of ¾ inch angle iron I got from my dad. The pegs were scrounged at Hurlbut's and the bar was held on with two "U" brackets.

The back pack used by Brian. Chain oil splotches are still evident on the straps!
(Photo 2018)

I learned from our East Coast trip to Boston the next year in 1974 that I mounted the sissy bar wrong. (Jeff's note—maybe our next book should be about that ride!) On the Cali trip I had the horizontal frame rod of the sissy bar under the turn signals. When I mounted it the next year, I put it over the turn signal. This made the sissy bar sit more vertical, which made sitting back against the stuff tied to the sissy bar much more comfortable with the standard handlebars.

I don't remember any cooking. We just camped a few times but ate at restaurants. I don't even remember carrying a canteen or water bottle. I ride with a water bottle always now. Mike and Jeff carried canteens. The only meal I clearly remember purchasing was in Grand Junction, CO, at a breakfast joint. Jeff and I had camped right off I-70 because it ended just west of town (two lanes across east California, NV and Utah) the night Mike decided to head back on his own to Nebraska. And we got breakfast the next morning in Grand Junction.

Luggage Bar—Mike

My bike was packed down so heavily that most people couldn't believe I could get all that "stuff" back on each morning or whenever I added injection oil to the Autolube tank. We didn't have the fancy luggage available now. I was using an official Boy Scout back pack with an aluminum frame.

Jeff's dad had made a short hoop like a sissy bar. It worked perfectly to bungee cord my back pack to it. If I did it right, I could lean back into that pack and get some support as I rode. The combination of my Z bars in front holding my sleeping bag to break the wind and my ability to lean back on the pack meant literally no muscle fatigue. That was important, especially when bucking a wind. I must have leaned on it a little too hard because the bar broke at the base on one side just before we got to Albuquerque.

Lucky for me, I made it to our destination in Albuquerque, and I could get the bar fixed before moving on to Phoenix. The bar never failed again.

Now, in the twenty-first century, I ride a 2001 FZ1 which actually sports a luggage rack from an R5. The set up looks better than anything made aftermarket, and I have carried so much stuff at a time including a sleeping bag, tent, compound bow, casserole, and a spare rim for my dad's boat in one trip. I worried I would get a ticket. One thing I learned on the 1973 trip was how to pack a bike.

That extended-fork 1970 R5 was extremely comfortable to ride. My machine had a few quirks, but it cornered surprisingly well and provided for a great perch! In fact, the last day of the trip, I traveled from the Colorado-Utah border to my eastern Nebraska home over 700 miles away.

Costs-Brian

We had to eat cheap because I think I did the whole trip, gas, food, everything for less than one hundred fifty dollars. Remember, we were young and skinny. But a tank of gas had to cost less than a dollar (this was before the oil embargo). Even a bottle of two-stroke oil was like sixty-nine cents. I also remember "cheating" a couple of times and adding regular four-stroke motor oil to the auto-oiler.

Costs—Mike

I don't have a clue about what things cost. I know I carried my billfold in my backpack most of the time on the way out, but in California, I got a pair of cargo jeans and loved the snap covers on the side pockets. After that, I never did sit on my billfold. When I got pulled over in LA by the CHP officer, I was asked for my driver's license. I turned to dig it out of my backpack. The officer, seeing me frantically rooting around and emotionally distressed, said sympathetically, "If it's in there, just forget it."

I carried everything I owned on me. Before we turned around and headed back to Nebraska while we were in LA, my mom gave me some money for the return trip. I came home so fast I didn't have time to spend much. My big expense was the Stetson Derby I purchased in Tahoe.

Riding, Thinking, Motion—Jeff

What does a guy think about cruising along on some droning two-stroke eight to ten hours a day? Forty-four years later, it is difficult to reconstruct my exact thoughts. As any motorcycle rider will tell you, much mental energy is put into monitoring the immediate situation: road conditions, intersections, wind conditions, oncoming traffic, and just the immediacy of the two-wheel experience. The motorcyclist must be alert, even after ten hours of riding. There is potential trouble ahead always.

But bikes are fun! Rounding curves is a joy, accelerating is exhilarating, and the profound connection a rider feels with his machine is very difficult to describe to non-riders. A person must experience the ride. Many of the large cruiser and touring bikes offered up for sale today have exotic entertainment and communication systems as well. Our situation was primitive compared to today, very open air, and environmentally immediate.

So, what did I think about while meandering down the highway to California back in 1973? Much of the time I was wondering how long it would be until I could get off that smoking, rattling beast and rest. I constantly measured and reviewed mileage and time goals in my head. A state on a highway map didn't look so big, and the red and blue road lines seemed easily doable. But the reality was different.

I thought about the weather and the wind constantly. We did not have fairings or windshields. The buffeting wind was a constant beat-down.

Yet, I was always excited to get through a town and return to the open highway. During our tedious sojourn through LA, we were intently focused on lane changes, signs, and speed limits. I relished twisty roads and slow climbs up forested mountains.

I have always been very sensitive to smells on the road. I thrilled at the aromas of the prairie, the ocean, and the western pines. It is amazing how distinct and fresh a newly-mown hayfield smells. On the other hand, it is equally amazing how pungent cigarette smoke could be when we were trailing a car with a live smoker!

I loved to see horses and cattle, swishing their tales, standing behind fences or stacks of hay. I loved deeply the sights and sounds of the desert, the prairies, the ocean, lakes, and rivers. While I was traveling in a group with my great friends, in many ways such a ride is a solitary experience. My thoughts fluctuated between concerns and great joys.

Of course, a person must spend a little time worrying about the motorcycles you are riding next to, in front of, or behind. We typically rode, if I remember correctly, in a flexible triangle formation with two bikes in the lead and one in the rear.

We were very trusting of each other, but time and mental energy was always being spent in riding safely in a formation, however loose it might be or become. We tried to develop some sophisticated hand signals to communicate. I think Mike and Brian were better at the hand signals than I was.

Mechanical issues and fueling issues and lubrication issues were always swirling around in my head somewhere. The Yamahas had a reserve gas range of about twenty-five to thirty miles. We could go a total of about one hundred twenty miles before refueling, so fill-ups always came around quickly. The chains had to be oiled and the Autolube oil injection system tanks had to be monitored and occasionally replenished.

I remember thinking off and on about the potential trouble of having a flat tire.

We carried along cold-patching kits for the tire inner tubes, but no one had a flat, thank goodness.

The possibility of piston seizure—complete mechanical failure when a piston welds itself to the cylinder—sometimes popped up in the dark recesses of my thoughts. But that never happened, either.

I didn't have a girlfriend, so I wasn't thinking about someone special or romance or movies or smooching. The pull of the west, and my focused quest to stand in the Pacific Ocean, well, that was my romance, my dream. I also knew, after seeing the oddities of San Francisco and the Bay Area, that it was time to go home, time to head back to the warm and loving prairie states, the place that seemed (to me, anyway) tangible and reality-based. And more romantic than California. Like Walt Whitman, I guess, I have always been connected to the poetry of my home. And though I have lived in Arizona most of my life, I can never forget the smell of the open prairies or the magnificent green order of the irrigated corn field.

I thoroughly enjoyed not studying for an exam or writing a paper while riding in the southwest and far west. I know I was prone to homesickness, and I thought a lot about finding a pay phone and calling home (collect) to see what was going on with my folks and sister. Brian and I, as you know, worked for a bee keeper at the time, and I know I was always a little concerned I would still have my bee job when I got back. Financial need for school was always gnawing at me, even two thousand miles away from home.

I know I saw myself as an adult, even though I clearly wasn't. I have always wanted to keep "the man" off my back, so I was constantly being careful to follow speed limits and warning signs. I might have had some music running in my head off and on, too, despite the wind noise and howling engines. Back then I was kind of a Top 40 guy—I liked songs by the Eagles ("Take It Easy," "Witchy Woman," and "Peaceful Easy Feeling") and some of the mushy stuff by Bread and Lobo and Chicago.

I enjoyed seeing my Aunt Deanna and Uncle Steve in Tempe, Arizona, and my maternal grandparents, Dr. Ray H. and Virginia Reynolds, in Phoenix. I know I thought a lot about wanting to see them but not bothering them.

The reader will notice below days or times on our trip when we didn't seem to do much except rest. I think that was particularly true when we visited Mike's mom in LA. We each have vivid memories of the ride across LA to her home on stilts, so to speak, in Woodland Hills. But our sight-seeing was limited that visit. No Disneyland, or Chinese Restaurant, or Dodger's game. The one-day ride from Phoenix to San Diego to LA through intense heat and traffic simply wore us out. LA was calling but we were beat.

Reflecting a little, I am still convinced we were more interested in the ride, the movement across prairie, desert, mountains, and forests, than we were with visiting iconic tourist destinations. But Team Black Rock did manage to take in the magnificent sights of San Francisco—at the apex of our journey. Things worked out just fine. Great people, great memories.

Riding Memories—Brian

On an open highway, with little traffic either direction, we would slalom between the middle-of-the-road dashed lines. The faster we would go, the more difficult it would be to sustain the accurate weaving.

Every one hundred to one hundred twenty miles, the two gallon-and-a-half gas tanks dictated a stop to refuel. This was therapeutic because the wind of the road and the two-stroke action necessitated a dismount and walk. Stretching was popular for us. I don't remember if it was cold in the morning very often (other than the mountains outside of San Diego after the desert crossing and in the Sierra Nevadas approaching and departing Yosemite). Early morning in Nevada and Colorado was cool. But no one complained about cold temperatures on this trip.

We used ear plugs (wadded up Kleenex or toilet paper, if I remember correctly). Keeping the noise down helped reduce the fatigue of four hundred to six hundred-mile days.

I wore gloves *all* the time, even in the heat of the desert. My hands were pearly white compared to my tanned arms. We always wore long jeans and boots. My riding wind-breaking coat was a button-up jean jacket with a hooded sweatshirt underneath. I remember it was adequate except for the rare chilly spots. Then, we just hurried on, there was nothing else to do except ride through it. I noted from the photos that I had a red, white, and blue visor I would don when I wasn't riding. I would open a bungee cord and secure it under the cord while riding. I considered myself cool when wearing it, and I faithfully wore it for the next couple of summers. I recall wishing that I had a full-face Bell helmet like Jeff and Mike. I picked up a blue visor in LA at a Kmart that I buttoned to the top of my face shield.

A topic of conversation was our speculation we could beat Harleys in a multi-hundred-mile race through mountains. We suspected they would surpass us in acceleration or top speed, but we were convinced we would beat them in the tight curves through mountains (nimble 350 Yamahas vs lumbering Milwaukee iron). Our passing and cornering on mountain corners became aggressive. We often would ignore the solid double yellow lines to pass a slower car coming out of a curve. I remember paying close attention to gravel in those corners and not accelerating too much (which would cause us to swing wide coming out of a corner, even going off the shoulder on occasion).

We used our horns to get the attention of one another as we would ride throughout the day. We frequently pointed out spots of scenic beauty or some activity going on next to the road or further inland. Being teenagers, we would check out occupants of cars as we would pass them or as they passed us. Our horn beeping and hand signaling would be very active for a few minutes after we saw a pretty girl. I believe our left-handed gesturing became sophisticated, and we could usually communicate our thoughts and comments quite clearly.

I sunburned the top-side of my left wrist where my watch was on that first afternoon driving to meet Mike in Beatrice. We couldn’t enjoy radio or tape-player music when we were riding (the technology wasn't there). We listened to music at a few of our stop-overs at friends. I remember Paul McCartney's James Bond theme song “Live and Let Die” when we toured San Francisco. Songs like Paul Simon's “Kodachrome,” Deep Purple’s “Smoke on the Water,” and Stephen Still’s “Love the One You’re With” were popular that summer.

Basic Itinerary

In chronological order, but not a perfectly detailed list, our fifteen-day trip went like this.... We left Beatrice, Nebraska, Thursday morning, June 20th.

.

First night—Camping in a rest area outside Dodge City, Kansas

Second night—Guests at Philmont Scout Ranch in New Mexico

Third night—Guests of Jeanette and her family in Albuquerque. We slept in a travel trailer next to the house.

Fourth and Fifth nights—We stayed with my grandparents, Dr. Ray and Virginia Reynolds, in Phoenix Arizona near 44th Street and Indian School. The three of us stayed in the back bedroom, which had a sliding glass door and easy access to the back-yard swimming pool. We would go out late at night and swim. Very exotic for three kids from Nebraska. My grandmother was a great cook, and I enjoyed her fried chicken so much!

Sixth and Seventh nights—We stayed with Mike's mom in Woodland Hills, California. I remember being quite exhausted after the long, hot ride from Phoenix on the sixth day. And the LA Freeway struggles!

Eighth night—Brian and I camped in Yosemite National Park. I think my ground cloth ended up being a blanket. And then there was that bear! Mike stayed a couple of extra days in Woodland Hills with his mom; he would catch up with us later in Vacaville.

Ninth and Tenth nights—Brian and I stayed in Vacaville, California with Judy and her family. We took an interesting day trip to San Francisco.

Eleventh night—Together again, the three of us stayed in a motel room (an expense!) in Ely, Nevada.

Twelfth night—Brian and I camped just off I-70 near Grand Junction, Colorado. Mike decided to head on home to Nebraska for his birthday, July 3rd.

Thirteenth night—Brian and I stayed with his uncle Bill and aunt Shirley Franzen in Denver. Now that was fun. We made it out to Golden Colorado with Brian's cousin Steve to sample the night life!

Fourteenth night—Back home in Nebraska on July 4th.

Highways—Jeff

I always have felt that Mike enjoys the prairies and the two-lane roads through cornfields and wind breaks best. Brian is a man of the Rockies. He enjoys the vistas, the forests, bubbling streams, and craggy peaks. Personally, for some reason, I have always enjoyed that big sky-open country feeling you get riding across New Mexico or far eastern Arizona. Some call that country the high prairies or high desert. That wonderful smell of prairies in the spring and the meadow lark songs still overpowers me. But we all enjoyed thc open road and the tug of distant horizons. Come on, man, it was 1973 and we were teenagers.

One of my favorite parts of our trip was the passage through the Salt River Canyon in central Arizona on Highway 60 between Show Low and Phoenix. This very scenic route (heading south) is composed of a six-mile-long series of downhill hairpin curves, crossing the Salt River over a scenic bridge, and then about five miles of uphill hair pin curves as you climb out of the valley back into a stretch of pine trees again, before beginning the long downhill scoot into Globe and the desert. There are some nice scenic vistas (turnouts) on both sides of the river. Back then there was a gas station at the bridge where you could buy fuel or add water to the radiator before making the long climb out of the canyon.

In 1973, the Interstate and freeway system wasn't fully complete. Sections of certain roads were still being built, especially concerning I-10 in Southern Arizona and I-70 in Utah and Colorado. The 5 and 405 in California were fully functional and challenging at times for us boys from Nebraska.

We took Highway 77 south of Beatrice down to I-70. We skated across Kansas till we took the 156 down through Great Bend and picked up the 56 to Kinsley. At that point, we headed down US 50 into Dodge City. From there, we picked up the 160 and travelled through Springfield, Colorado into Trinidad.

Then we headed south on I-25 until we veered southwest off on US 64 to Philmont Scout Ranch.

The next portion of our trip took us through Red River and Taos then down I-25 to Albuquerque.

Heading south to Socorro, we turned west on US 60 for the 350 miles or so to Phoenix.

We left Phoenix on a very hot morning in June and wandered through city streets until we got to Buckeye and picked up State Route 85 at Buckeye and headed south to Gila Bend and Interstate 8. We headed west across barren desert through Yuma and across the Colorado River and eventually reached San Diego.

Team Black Rock took Interstate 5 north out of San Diego but got lost and separated several times. We probably travelled on I-5, I-405, I-805, and several other derivatives of the California Interstate system north bound, which existed in 1973. At one point, a CHP officer stopped Brian and me to help us get reunited with Mike. The officer, noticing our Nebraska license plates, gently advised us it might be best to return to the flatlands as soon as possible. Undaunted, or at least stubborn, we did reach Woodland Hills in the LA area just at dark.

Brian and I left Woodland Hills by eventually picking up the I-5 and heading north until we came into Kings County and moved off onto California 41 N, which eventually took us through Fresno and then to Yosemite National Park.

From Yosemite, we took 120 Highway to the California 99 and numerous county roads and farm roads, then on to Vacaville. (Mike met up with us in Vacaville. He had stayed in LA to visit with his mom for a couple of extra days.)

On our return trip, we took I-80 across California from Vacaville, found our way around Lake Tahoe, and picked up US 50 again (eastbound) through Ely, Nevada. Heading east and homeward bound, we meandered down Highway 6 and did a little jog on the I-15 (US 91) South of Provo and picked up the I-70. We went through Grand Junction to Denver. From Denver, we moved up I-80S (now I-76) until we connected with I-80 and rolled on into Nebraska as far as Aurora. We sort of had multiple home-pathways at that point. Mike and Brian and I explain our final "solo" miles below. But we all made it to our homes (in York and Beatrice) safely and had a terrific experience!

III

Let's Ride!

Kansas—Mike

We had a heck of a sendoff from Beatrice, Nebraska. I have a few memories of the party. Mass quantities of beer were consumed by people. Nebraska was a "19" state back then. I'm sure that I drank Dr. Pepper. I gave Pam (now my wife) my class ring and told her I would be back. I had met her only two days earlier. Positively love at first sight! The house where we had the party is still standing in Beatrice.

The three of us, Team Black Rock, left Beatrice and rode to Dodge City, Kansas the first day of the trip.

For some reason, we made a quick stop right after we left Beatrice, the first morning, in Wymore, Nebraska, to see the guy who had bought the '68 Charger from me.

Jeff and Brian in Wymore Nebraska. Mike's chopped R5 is to the left.

We had a little rain further south, near Salina Kansas. But there wasn't much rain the whole trip. That first couple of hundred-mile days we just got acclimated to riding as a trio and then droned along under mostly clear Midwest summer skies. Were we excited? You bet! I remember we would take turns accelerating and passing each other and acting kind of goofy.

We slept out in the open on a roadside rest area just east of Dodge. While we were resting, a gentleman rode up on a big touring bike and talked with us. He said, "See that factory over there? That's mine." He promised to send a state patrolman to check on us, and so he did. I slept on a concrete picnic table because I was afraid of rattlesnakes. I don't remember much for a while after that except eating at an A&W for lunch the next day.

Jeff at Rest Area near Dodge City, Kansas

Somewhere in West Kansas June 1973. Note the tie-downs on gear.

I have no idea exactly where the following happened, but we were in some God-forsaken area which was flat as hell. We were cruising a long, lonely stretch of foothills prairie highway. This was one of those spots on the map where we had just enough fuel capacity to make it to the next town. Because of the longer fork tubes, my tank was angled up. This kept me from using all the gas in my tank. I had already switched to reserve way before Jeff and Brian did. I could see a small town in the distance when my bike sputtered a few times and died. They came back, realized what happened, and decided to continue into the town, promising to return with gas for me.

Time passed. I thought I had waited long enough, and I decided I better start to help myself. I leaned the Yamaha to the left, hoping to drain the remaining fuel into the petcock and fill my carb bowls. My plan worked. I started the bike up, ran it through the gears, shut it off, and coasted as far as I could. I repeated the process till I made it to the only gas station in town. A gas pump stood on the left side of the street by the sidewalk. Next to the pump sat two black and orange R5s. I went inside to find my buddies sitting peacefully on some worn out looking chairs. I bought a cold Dr. Pepper and paused for a second.

Jeff brought me up to speed: "Due to the gas shortage, they won't sell us any gas." Their reasoning? "If we sell you our gas, we won't have any for ourselves." I thought about it for a while, and when my soda was gone, I asked the station owner if there was any place to stay and if there were any jobs available in town. He asked me why, and I explained if we weren't going anywhere, we would need jobs and a place to stay. That's when one of the other bib overall-wearing gents said, "Aww sell the boys some gas." Like a cat playing with a mouse, they became bored with us and decided to let us go. We filled up and rode out. A most interesting event during our trip.

Center Stand Issues—Mike

Since my Yamaha was altered with the ten-inch longer fork tubes, the side stand didn't function very well. I just didn't have time to alter it before the trip. It was a little tipsy, but the center stand would support the bike. Well, most of the time. Everything went well until we parked in this freshly-asphalted parking lot in the hot sun somewhere in west Kansas.

The "customization design" finally caught up to me. I think we had gone in to catch a bite at a diner or Dairy Queen, but when we came out, my Yamaha was lying on Brian's motorcycle. His machine had saved mine from a catastrophic fall. At first glance, it looked like both bikes survived without issues, but there was a problem. My clutch lever had caught the seat cover of his Yamaha and tore a small patch of his seat.

Brian was clearly upset. I didn't blame him. I mean, the Yamaha was his pride and joy. As was mine. A solution was soon reached. We simply pulled pins and switched the seats. Mine was now his and his, with the tear, was now mine. I lived with it, contrite. After that, whenever we stopped, I placed an old tennis shoe under the stand to give my bike the extra length and "footprint" required so it wouldn't sink into the soft asphalt. And, I had to park a little farther away. Or—at least on the left side of everyone else.

New Mexico—Mike

We enjoyed staying in Philmont Scout Camp. Brian had worked there the previous summer as a Boy Scout. We were welcomed by the scouts, and they gave us a tent to stay in. It was very nice and had a wood pallet floor. We ate with them and went to town in an old school bus to watch a movie, a black and white film called *The Last Picture Show.* We paid a minimal fee at the ticket window, but the real surprise occurred when we walked into the theater. A fire had occurred recently, and the roof was gone. The experience was surreal. We were watching this movie in black and white while sitting in the ruins of a theater and looking up from the screen to see all the stars in the sky. A moment in time I will never forget.

Red River, New Mexico—Mike

Brian knew of this special place—a New Mexico resort town full of wealthy people at a higher elevation. The area was covered with mature pine trees and had a beautiful stream coming down out of the mountains. This was a posh locale for tourists to come and play. And we did. Brian took us to a building where we could rent motorcycles by the hour and run around town. We acquired the latest Honda SL70s. All the colors were available, including red, blue, and gold. They were just scaled-down versions of my friend Dave's SL100 back home in Nebraska.

(The one I stuck in the crotch of a tree on an early morning ride with his brother Dennis. We were jumping an abandoned rail road track to see who could fly the highest. We would take turns and one would spot at the top and hold his hand up to where the back tire had crossed his chest. The jump was in a wooded area with trees on both sides. We had to be careful not to hit a tree. All was going great, with each of us getting chest high or so, when it happened. Something went wrong, and I got crossed up on the trail we were using. To this day, I don't know exactly how this happened, but I did it.

I landed that SL100 right smack dab in the crotch of a tree on the other side. I didn't try to do it, but I stuck it perfectly. The bike was balanced upright, and I was still on it with my feet on the pegs. The frame was wedged in the tree. Crazy. The look on Dennis' face was total shock. "What do we do now?" I said. Dennis just laughed. "Leave it. Tell Dave he did it last night. He might not remember." So, we did. God, I wish I had a picture of that motorcycle wedged in the branches.)

Back to Red River. The operator of the dirt bike rental business offered, "I guess you all know how to ride, and I guess I don't need to rent you any helmets." So, after paying the man, off we went. Each of us pulled a wheelie as we left. We didn't look back. Brian led us through town, and then he turned off the main road. Before long, we were rid of the pavement.

We came up to the lovely stream, flowing down the mountain, which wasn't very big or deep right then, just fast. Brian went first. He dropped the clutch and launched that bike right into the stream. He had crossed about half way when he hit a boulder under the water. I don't know whether the rock rolled to the side when he caught it with his front tire or if his wheel just slipped off, but the result was he was lying sideways in the stream before anybody knew what happened. Jeff was right behind him. He navigated the creek successfully, but when he got to the other side, the bank was too steep. He lost traction, slipped back into the water, and the bike stalled.

Of course, I was closest to Jeff. I watched and learned. I navigated past Brian as he was standing in the current holding his Honda by the handlebars. I chose another place to get out on the opposite bank. I was successful. I put the SL70's side stand down on a firm spot. I waded in to help Jeff with his SL70, and then we both went in to get Brian's bike out. We all had a good laugh.

After we had the bikes on the other side of the stream, we were surprised at how easily they started and immediately ran perfectly. A tribute to the people at Honda, I'm sure. We hopped on and raced through the trees, zig-zagging up the mountain. I felt like I was in an episode of *The Monkees* TV show. Great fun. Once we got to the top, we found a road which took us down the hill way too fast. Team Black Rock took the SL70s back to the rental office and got the heck out of there. Everybody should have such an experience at least once in their lives. That was a blast!

Brian's Sleeping Bag—Mike

Somewhere in the high country of New Mexico, probably north of Santa Fe, the scenery was beautiful. I was following the guys, hanging back like I often did because I enjoyed watching the two bikes in front of me. However, I often followed Jeff and Brian for a simple reason. My sleeping bag was strapped to my handlebars to provide a kind of windbreak, and the bag obscured my speedometer and tachometer. So, I stayed behind the other two because I couldn't tell how fast I was going. I depended on them to set the pace at the proper speed.

Anyway, the day was late, and traffic seemed very heavy. The sun was edging lower in the western sky. We wanted to quit riding for the day, but there were still a few miles to go. Then, suddenly, I don't know what caused it, or why it happened, but Brian's sleeping bag just shot off his bike. I think it must have shifted from his leaning against it or something, but the thing just launched, bounced a few times, and rolled to a stop off to the side of the road in a ditch.

We pulled over immediately, and since it was Brian's equipment, he had to negotiate the traffic and go back to retrieve the runaway sleeping bag. Those were a tense few minutes, but nothing Brian couldn't handle. He bungeed the bag back on and we continued our way to Albuquerque.

From York, Nebraska, to Phoenix, Arizona-Brian

The first day of the trip, when Jeff and I rode from York down to Beatrice to meet up with Mike, I forgot to take my watch off my wrist. The next day, I had a good sunburn right where the watch rested. No amount of sunscreen could protect my wrist for the rest of the trip. I applied sunscreen liberally thereafter, but the sunburn blistered and never completely healed for three weeks. I would ride for long periods holding onto the mirror support, which provided shade to my sunburned wrist (and tanned my inner arm).

After our first full day of riding from Nebraska into Kansas, we camped at a rest area outside of Dodge City, Kansas, along US 50. No problem. No concerns for our safety or decision. Today, in 2019, we would probably be arrested for camping in such a place. Back then, we just rolled out our bags by a picnic table and spent the night.

Kansas/Colorado border heading west

The next day, we went past Springfield, Colorado and just before turning south toward Pritchet, Colorado, Mike's bike ran out of gas (due to the extended forks that prevented him from fully utilizing the reserve gas in his fuel tank). Jeff and I kept riding into town before we realized Mike wasn't with us. We turned back and I pushed him into Pritchet by nudging his bike along with my right foot pressed against his left rear shock absorber.

We rode to Philmont Scout Ranch outside Cimarron, New Mexico. (I worked there the previous summer.) We had tent and cot accommodations and got a couple of nice meals and showers because I knew some of the guys at Philmont. I also had an opportunity to visit with some of my old ‘colleagues’ from the camp.

Mike and Jeff at Philmont

Brian and Jeff at Philmont

Then, we headed to Albuquerque. We headed west on Highway 54 from Cimarron to Eagles Nest and on to Red River, NM. We rented little Honda motorcycles and thrashed the mountain roads around Red River. Back on the Yamahas, Team B continued through Taos then down I-25 to Albuquerque where we stayed with my friend Jeanette (who I got to know the previous summer, at Red River, when I worked at Philmont) and her folks. Jeanette and I were good friends, but I never saw her again after we rode out of Albuquerque.

Jeff, Mike, and I slept out in a small travel trailer. Jeanette was into listening to the Johnny Winter *Live* album and Cream. Johnny Winter was playing a live concert in Albuquerque that summer, and his band was a very hot local topic. We took Jeanette and two of her girlfriends on the back of our bikes down I-25 to a mall or someplace after dark. I didn't feel very safe riding on the highway not wearing a helmet (with a face shield) and with a passenger behind me.

Mike, Jeanette, and Jeff in Albuquerque the morning we left

Later, well into Arizona, we enjoyed riding down the switchbacks heading into Salt River Canyon, and then ripping back up the canyon curves—a great time on the Yamahas.

Salt River Canyon Between Show Low and Globe AZ US Highway 60

You go down about ten miles, curves everywhere, cross the Salt River Bridge at the bottom, then go up through wonderful twisties again for another five or six miles and exit the canyon. Jeff tells me the road has been improved since then, but US 60 through the Salt River Canyon in 1973 was a real blast for bikes! This is where I lost fifth gear. My bike just wouldn't “find the gear” when I shifted into fifth, so I stayed in fourth gear as high gear the rest of the trip.

When we were east of Phoenix, we rolled through Globe, Arizona. Not a pretty town. Globe was a mining town. Rich in history, though. Billy the Kid apparently rustled some cattle around there in 1877 or so. I believe the last stagecoach robbery in American history happened, back in 1899, near Globe, too. I recall the city was hot and dusty as we drove past the big open-pit mine.

Somewhere after Globe, still on Highway 60, during the late afternoon, probably near Superior and the Bluebird Mine area, we were riding through some pitched and curvy section of the highway when a blue VW Beetle (the old-fashioned Beetle) swerved into my lane and nearly took me out. We had been gazing into the sun and moving in and out of patches of shade created by the canyon walls. Good thing I saw that Beetle and avoided a crash. That rattled us a little bit, and we had to pull over and regroup before riding the last forty miles or so into Phoenix.

We made it to Phoenix and enjoyed the hospitality of Jeff's grandparents. They lived near 40th Street and Indian School at the time. We also appreciated their air-conditioning and swimming pool. Just outside the sliding door in the room where we slept was their swimming pool, which was so cool to have so close. We swam a lot, even after dark. I was impressed by the low berms surrounding their entire lot—both front and back yards. The berms were used to contain water used to irrigate their lawn and trees. But other than swimming, we pretty much stayed indoors and rested and avoided the heat.

We did get out to visit a motorcycle shop. As I mentioned, I had lost fifth gear on my motorcycle someplace during the Salt River Canyon run. I would keep up in fourth gear ok, but a higher RPM multiplied the vibration and the engine whine. I got a larger-count counter-shaft sprocket at Apache Cycles in Mesa, Arizona which trimmed the higher RPM a little bit for the rest of the trip. (I didn't want to get the transmission overhauled at this point of the trip—time, work, and money!) This was a clever solution and dropped the rpms to a suitable level at sixty-five mph. I believe this was the only mechanical issue we suffered on the trip, other than Mike's occasional low gas problem. While we were in Mesa, we also visited Jeff's aunt and uncle, Deanna and Steve Cooley.

Albuquerque and more—Jeff

We spent the night in a travel trailer, or maybe it was a camper shell on jacks, in Albuquerque. The trailer was parked, next to Jeanette's house, on a concrete driveway or apron. At some point in the late evening, Team Black Rock was sitting out on lawn chairs just outside the trailer. The three girls were inside the trailer whispering about witches and brujas and ghosts! After things settled down, we could call it a night. No, the trailer was not haunted. Fun.

The ride south from Albuquerque to Socorro and then west to Arizona is interesting. Lots of open high desert, rolling hills, and big skies. I-25 runs near the Rio Grande River and heads south to the city of Socorro. (Why Socorro? "Socorro" means "help" in Spanish. Apparently, a group of worn-out Spanish settlers were given water and food here by local indigents in 1598. The settlement then received its event-marking name: Socorro). At Socorro, motorists can pick up US 60. There are several picturesque New Mexico villages along the way, including Quasimodo, Pie Town, and Magdalena. At the time, the Very Large Array radio telescope installation was being built about fifty miles west of Socorro. We didn't see any of the large dish radio telescopes back then that dot the landscape today. We just noticed bulldozers, trucks, and surveyors. US 60 West across New Mexico, while scenic and peaceful, is brutal in one respect. A vicious head wind is usually blowing during the spring and summer months.

Arizona has several climate zones: high plateau in the northern third, forest in the middle, and desert in the south. Elevations and scenery change abruptly. Steep mountain grades and brake check turn-outs abound. A totally interesting place, seldom mentioned, is Gonzales Pass, about seven miles west of Superior on US 60.

After rolling along at 2500 feet elevation on a curvy mountain road or so for several miles, you suddenly crest the pass and then can look out across the burning Sonoran Desert toward Phoenix. The flat landscape, and dusty haze, and sporadic desert peaks rising from the desert floor, especially when gazing into the late afternoon summer sun, provide for a stunning vista. And as you descend on a motorcycle, the rise in temperature as you drop 1000 feet or so is very noticeable. Into the furnace!

Gonzales Pass Looking toward Phoenix area (courtesy Pass Bagger)

From Phoenix to San Diego to LA- Mike

We left Phoenix early in the morning after taking advantage of the Reynolds' private pool for a couple of days. That was a relaxing time in Arizona, even though it was terrifically hot outside. The desert heat is relentless. We first noticed the warm air at the bottom of the Salt River Canyon a few days earlier. We spent a little time wandering around Thomas Mall and a lot more time swimming in the pool. Each day was always hot. The temp was ninety-five degrees at 9:30 am the morning we left Phoenix.

During this portion of the trip, Brian's foot peg adhesive let go and the foot peg slid off in heavy traffic somewhere in Phoenix or Avondale or Buckeye. There was nothing I could do as I watched the black rubber peg bounce all over the road. We just couldn't stop to retrieve it safely.

So, on we went. (Brian bought a replacement at a California motorcycle shop later). Mid-day found us riding three abreast as we sometime did for fun, out on the open road. We savored the sound of three R5s doing sixty side-by-side, moaning and setting up a mesmerizing harmonic wail. I sometimes nodded off briefly. That shook me up. In the heat, you just kind of sweated and hung on and lusted for water and shade.

When we got to San Diego, we just kept going west, whatever it took, just kept going west. Then we were there. The sun and surf. The ocean! We shut off our bikes at the beach parking lot. The two-stroke rattle was suddenly replaced by the sounds of people enjoying a summer day at the beach. Brian and Jeff, I thought, had never seen the ocean. They parked their bikes quickly and ambled towards the sea. They headed straight down to the water's edge wearing jackets, jeans, and all. I didn't want to leave my Yamaha, so I stayed put.

Some small kid with sun-bleached hair ran up to me while I was standing in the lot and exclaimed, "Somebody stole my surfboard! Have you seen any cops?" No, I hadn't seen any cops. Sort of a strange welcome, don't you think?

While the guys were enjoying fun in the sun and the ocean spray, I fiddled with my bike and topped off the oil. I re-adjusted my sleeping bag. I carried it on the handlebars and gauges, using the roll like a fairing. I would place my map folded on top the bag with the route showing and marked up with notes, as to which way to turn, beside the map. The system worked well. But that day, when I re-attached the bag, I accidentally pinched the throttle cable. Then, when I gave the starter a kick, the motor went WIDE OPEN THROTTLE! There was no kill switch on the handlebars in those days, and I had to reach under the tied-down sleeping bag to get to the key and turn the engine off! My mind was racing and so was the motor. I was thinking: "This is as far from home as I can get, and I just destroyed my motor." Thankfully, I didn't. After finding the cable problem and correcting the issue, the bike started right off and idled correctly. The R5 was fine. But that episode could have been a disaster.

The San Diego Beach—Jeff

Yes, it was a long, hot ride through Arizona to Yuma and extreme southern California. There just isn't much to see—not many large cacti or communities. Just simmering sand and bristly brown mountains etched against the ever-present white-hot sky. The saguaro cactus population begins to thin after Gila Bend (once known as the Fan Belt Capital of the World), and the Sonoran Desert takes on more of a Middle Eastern quality. Sand dunes stretch along the edge of I-8 between Yuma and El Centro, and the desert is quite bare. El Centro, CA, is about fifty feet below sea level.

Those Algodones Dunes along the freeway are quite scenic, but this area is very different than the Sonoran Desert back around Gila Bend and Phoenix. There just aren't as many cactus (like the saguaro and ocotillo) and desert trees (like the Palo Verde and mesquite) down there in the extreme SW corner of Arizona and southern border of California. Phoenix averages maybe seven and a half inches of rain a year. El Centro, CA, is probably lucky to see three inches.

Rolling along at sixty-five mph on a motorcycle in the desert heat does not provide for a cooling wind. Think of falling asleep with your face near a blasting electric space heater.

Things got better as we rolled through the coastal mountains east of San Diego, but the traffic picked up, too. California coastline's beauty is well-documented. Hard to say exactly how we found the beach in San Diego. But there it was—my first sight of the ocean. Of course, I was impressed, just as I am today when I visit the coast and gaze westward across the blue expanse.

Not worried about getting my flared-bottom jeans wet, I took my boots and socks off and walked along the water's edge in amazement. This was a bit of an error since I then had irritating dry sand stuck to my socks later as we rode northward to LA. But during those brief moments at the beach, the sights and sounds of the gentle ocean waves and marine haze and seabirds and the people in the water—well, all of this was pure magic for me.

I also heard a two-stroke motorcycle screaming in the distance. That's Mike's story.

North to LA—Mike

The next moto-trek was to LA. On a Friday afternoon, our LA freeway was busy. We were forced into the space of a single car and it wasn't fun. After a few hours, we managed to pull off and get to a gas station, top off fuel, and have a soda. On the way in, a local dude on a beautiful Harley chopper followed us and asked us if we just got off the freeway. I said, "Yeah, and that's why we are here now, to let the traffic die down a bit and get back on. He said, "Man, I live here, and I won't go on the freeway this time of day." We complimented him on his nice ride, and we got along great and then went our separate ways.

Right now, I need to let you know my mother lived in the LA basin in Woodland Hills, but I had never been to her house. All I had was the address on a piece of paper.

Traffic was still bad that Friday evening hours later when I realized we needed to get off the freeway at a certain exit to go to her house. I methodically veered off down the exit, but the guys didn't follow me on the ramp. Now I had to act quickly or lose them forever. They didn't have her address written down anywhere, a big mistake on our part. As you know, we didn't have cell phones in those days. I cut across the grass on top of the on ramp and headed back to the busy freeway to catch them. I guess you could say I did a little motocross on my chopper! I didn't go far before I was pulled over by a CHP officer on a motorcycle. Things were not looking good.

When he asked for my driver's license, I started digging in my back pack behind me. He asked if I really was from Nebraska, and I said, "Yes." He said, "Oh no, were those other two guys with you?" "Yes." "OK, I'll go ahead and pull them over. You just keep going on this road till you catch up with us." I'll bet that was maybe a twenty-minute ride, but the experience felt like an hour. Sure enough, I caught up with them. They were parked along the road watching cars zoom by.

We never talked about it, but I'm not sure if those two ever missed me or realized they were lost.

Woodland Hills, California, June 1973

When we got close to mom's house up in the Woodland Hills canyons, I thought we could just figure out the directions maze, but it was harder than I thought. I saw a lady with her two children playing in their yard. I stopped the bike, lifted off my full-face helmet, and said, "Excuse me Ma'am," and that was all it took. She jumped up and grabbed her two kids in her arms and ran in the house screaming. I didn't know I had such an effect on people. To say the least, that was unexpected.

So, we went back down to a 7-Eleven convenience store we had passed earlier to ask for directions. We got them from a nice clerk and finally found mom's house. When I told mom what happened with the lady and her children and asked her why the lady reacted so strangely, she said that Steve McQueen lived just up the canyon and he had a lot of parties and invited all kinds of bikers. He got along fine with them. But some of the neighbors were a little skittish about dudes on motorcycles. Must have been great parties!

Mom's house was built off the side of the canyon. I swear only one wall was on solid ground. The rest was supported by steel beams sunk into rock. I didn't care. From the small deck on the back of the house, you were suspended in space. I could easily see the neighbor's pool in their back yard. And it looked tiny from up there!

Oh. At first, when we found her house, strangely enough, the electricity was out. I remember how spooky it was when I heard a Korat cat (a gray cat with a raspy meow and bright green eyes) for the first time in a dark house that stuck out from the side of a steep canyon. Mom had about twenty exotic cats which she took to various shows.

After getting the lights working again, I checked out the back deck of the house. Looking down, that's when I spotted the tiny pool in the neighbor's yard. Suddenly tired and a bit overwhelmed, I realized I had experienced enough for one day. I went back inside.

Phoenix and California—Brian

When we left Phoenix, we added additional two-stroke oil to our gas tanks as preventative medicine in preparation for riding two-strokes across the flaming desert. We didn't want them to seize up in the intense heat. As an aside, my daughter and son-in-law lived in Buckeye, west of Phoenix, in the early 2000s. One day while visiting them, we drove into downtown Buckeye, and the trip seemed a *Déjà vu* moment for me. The downtown area wasn't much improved, probably because I-10 had been built about six miles north of there, drawing most of the through-traffic away from downtown. It just seemed like I had been there before, which I had, back in the summer of 1973.

Team Black Rock took a long time to get out of Phoenix. Then the ride was very hot through Gila Bend. Just open desert and distant mountains. We stopped in Yuma for quite a while to cool off. That sounds kind of funny, doesn't it? "Cooling off in Yuma?"

Later that morning (we left very early in the morning, before the sun was up), I remember heading through the mountains east of San Diego and thinking how chilly it was, compared to the desert ride earlier in the day. I put my full jean jacket and sweatshirt on due to the brisk air.

As we drove into San Diego, we stayed on the freeway to the very end of the road. We literally drove right up to the ocean and parked our bikes and then, in jeans and boots, we walked through the sandy beach right to the water. A pretty amazing experience.

After a time, we headed on up the coast to LA to see Mike's mom.

The ride into LA was somewhat scary, for a young Nebraskan not used to so much traffic, on five or six lanes of freeway. There were some issues, for sure. We took an exit for gas in a not-so-nice neighborhood. And we got separated on the freeway. I casually looked right and saw Mike heading down the exit ramp, and I wondered, with concern, how we would ever meet up again. (Mike tells that story.)

Later, the LA haze we saw from Mike's mom's house was noticeable (again, something not common for a Cornhusker). In 1974, Jimmy Buffet came out with his first hit single "Come Monday," and it included the phrase "in a brown LA haze." That song, with that phrase, even today, reminds me of that trip. Mike's mom's house was on a hillside, supported by "stilts," which fascinated me. I had never seen that architectural style before. Riding through the twisty roads of the LA canyons was fun.

We went to a Kmart in LA and I purchased a blue visor that buttoned onto my helmet face shield (which I thought was cool...).

North to Yosemite—Brian

After resting a couple of days in LA, and not doing much, Jeff and I continued northward. (Mike stayed for a longer visit with his mom and they eventually trailered his bike to Vacaville). Our trip would take us to Yosemite National Park and then to Vacaville to visit one of my friends. We drove up I-5, to the point where we cut east to head to Yosemite. I remember thinking California was a long state during our I-5 ride.

Yosemite

Jeff in Yosemite

I thought riding through Yosemite on bikes was surreal, seeing Half Dome, the Valley, and so much more. Trees and the other scenery in Yosemite were magnificent. Later, when we were camping and I was calling my mom from a phone booth, a large black bear came into view. Suddenly, Jeff "joined me" in the phone booth! Yes, he was afraid of that bear!

The ride from Yosemite to Vacaville was through farming and wine country. Some of the vineyards were framed by mountains, which was very picturesque. The many rivers and irrigation canals stick in my mind. That section of the trip wasn't a very direct ride, as we did lots of cutting back and forth on roads, stopping often to look at the map and figuring out where to go. Jeff and I traveled all two-lane highway and county roads; no Interstate travel was involved. After leaving the mountains, the farm country was very warm.

Judy and Robert in Vacaville

When we got to Vacaville, we stopped at a Safeway (or some chain grocery store) to see if we could meet my friend Judy's father, who worked at the store as a butcher, to get directions. I don't remember whether we connected with him or not. But we found our way to her house in Vacaville. Her brother, Robert, was playing Stephen Stills' "Love the One You're With" that summer on his acoustic guitar. I thought Robert, who was a year or two younger than us, would turn into another friend. I liked how he could play guitar and sing (that one song).

On the first full day after our arrival, we all went to a lake outside of Vacaville. We enjoyed swimming and splashing in the water and eating a picnic lunch. That was a fun trip. At the lake, I sensed Judy wanted to take our friendship a notch higher, but I remember Jeff and Robert were hanging out together, having fun in the lake, and I wanted to join those guys rather than build the relationship with Judy. Kind of weird.... But her family was very nice, very hospitable.

Staying Behind in Woodland Hills—Mike

While Jeff and Brian went to Yosemite and Vacaville and San Francisco, I stayed in LA to visit with my mom for a couple of days. At her insistence, I rented a small U-Haul and trailered my bike to Vacaville. I pulled the set-up with her baby blue Ford Pinto.

When I unloaded the bike, I thought the R5 was ready to go, but one of the new Nippon Denso plugs I had installed back at mom's fouled immediately. I installed a used Champion and I just left them in there till I got home. Those R5s didn't require a lot of maintenance, but there was always something to do.

San Francisco—Brian

On the second day in Vacaville, we took a day trip by car to San Francisco. The city was amazing. We took in the significant sights like Ghirardelli Square, Fisherman's Wharf, and the Fairmont Hotel. Of course, we rode on a street car in a very hilly area and enjoyed street food all over town. We went up the outside glass elevator to the top of the Fairmont Hotel for a view over the city. We didn't have elevators, especially outside glass elevators in York, so riding it to the top of the building was special. We enjoyed portrait artists, a mime, a cool Sterling Car, and gazing at Alcatraz Island across the harbor.

RALPH

San Francisco June 1973

San Francisco was a real cultural treat for us. Those few hours of driving to San Francisco and back also included the most radio music we listened to for the entire trip. Hits like Paul Simon's "Kodachrome" and

Paul McCartney's "Live and Let Die," the then-current James Bond movie's theme song, were on the "heavy" play list on the AM stations in the Bay area (and across America). Again, the sights in San Francisco were special to us. That's why I took that photo of the yellow Sterling sports car. There weren't cars like that in York County, Nebraska!

Someone obviously touched my butt when we were riding in a crowded cable car. About that same time, I remember Jeff making eye contact with me. He had a surprised or concerned look on his face. Jeff confided to me, later that day, that he had also been strangely touched while riding on the street car. Oh, well. That was part of a fun West Coast excursion.

I don't remember riding away from Judy's house in Vacaville. Did you notice, from the photos, all the late sixties, early seventies cars on the street? That's what was going on then.

Mike and Jeff Conversing Before Leaving Vacaville CA

Nevada to Colorado to Nebraska—Mike

Lake Tahoe was an oasis after the deserts and high chaparral we had ridden through. Here is this beautiful lake in the middle of what seemed like a desert. All kinds of boats were out on the water. Sail boats vectored out in the middle of the place and a beautiful speed boat with a chromed-out V8 engine sticking out the back zoomed along the shore. A loud exhaust was coming straight out of the chrome headers. Oh, and did I mention there were lots of motorcycles? Mostly Harleys and such. They didn't like my R5 with the Z bars and ten-inch tubes. I found a place where I bought my only souvenir, a black Stetson Derby. I packed that baby on the back of my bike all the way home.

Two guys in a '65 or '66 Chevy 4-door Impala pulled up beside me. They had the windows down, and in the back seat sat a large German Shepherd with his head sticking out, barking loudly. The dog was trying to reach out and bite me as they crowded me with their car. They were laughing. I didn't think much of it, though. Later that day, as we were taking it all in, we talked to a police officer. He said crime was quite a problem in the Tahoe area.

I heard a big, bearded, tattooed Harley guy yell at me, "Someone chopped a f***ing mosquito!" Well, that about did it. I dropped a couple of gears and headed for the highway. I was done with lovely Tahoe. I convinced Jeff and Brian now was our time to go. Even though late in the day, we left.

At some point after leaving Tahoe, we rode into a small town just off the highway. The place looked like a ghost town or some sad, bleak place featured in a movie. We were in the middle of a desert. Strangely, a little kid on a dirt bike led us into town. I remember lunch was good. But something was eerie about the kid and the locale. No, we were not in Area 51.

Lake Tahoe late June 1973

Tahoe and Crossing Nevada and Utah—Brian

We rode out to Lake Tahoe. I remember I was on a mission to buy a California t-shirt, in the last California town we would be in. The theme and message on the t-shirt I bought was kind of dumb, but I wore the shirt proudly for many years in memory of our great trip. We parked our bikes and went over to the beach, but the water was quite cold and the sand on the beach was obviously slanted, not flat.

Then we launched into Nevada. I remember Nevada was a “vacant” state with lots of vistas and distant mountains on the horizon. We’d do a long, straight-line multi-mile valley drive and then launch into a set of mountain curves and passes. Seems like we took a long time to cross the state. But we enjoyed “Spudnuts” in either Ely or Eureka. Spudnuts were donuts made from potato flour. Again, something I had never experienced! Spudnuts were made or distributed in one of those towns, and we had to try them.

Utah was a surprisingly tough state to drive through from west to east. There wasn't a straight-through highway. The roads seemed much more north/south oriented. To make progress heading east, we took many north/south highways with different numbers. We had to use our maps a lot that day. I-70 was partially built in eastern Utah. We rode across Nevada and Utah on sections of Highway 50 and Highway 6, which of course, was a major highway in our part of Nebraska. When Jeff and I were working bees, much of the travel was on and around our old highway friend, US 6, in south-central Nebraska.

The Norton Commando—Mike

Back then, and still to this day, if you had a Norton Commando, a British vertical twin motorcycle, you were somebody special. The three of us were on a two-lane highway headed through Utah. Suddenly, a guy on a 750 Commando, who was lying down on the tank, blew by us like we were anchored. Jeff was in the lead of our group at that moment. He raised his left hand and waved us into action.

We had become pretty good with our hand signal communications by then, but I thought we couldn’t pull this one off. How could we catch that rocket?

Well, we maneuvered into a line and, I think, thanks to the draft, we just slipstreamed the Norton. He pulled us along and we hung with the show-off with little effort. Those howling 350s appeared quite up to the task. A while down the road, he sat up to check his mirror and he got an eye full of three Yamaha R5s right on his tail! Once he knew we were still with him, we raised up, parachute-style, and backed off, letting him go with a wave. Point proven!

Colorado—Mike

After a few more hours of riding, they motioned me to pull off on an exit ramp in far western Colorado. This was at a construction site. I-70 was being built/expanded in that area at the time. They wanted to put up a tent and sleep right along the highway. I said no way, not there. I was going home. I was going to ride on. All night if I had to, but I wasn't stopping. We parted company. Our dusk exit ramp parley was the end of our trip in terms of the three of us riding together.

I went on. I had to stop for gas, but everything was closed. I had no credit card, but I found a prepay gas pump. I had to put in $5.00 and got only about $1.50 worth of fuel. I hated that, but it was the only way to keep going. I was foolish to try to keep going. I had no real map and only a medium-blue face visor (not so good for night vision). Of course, it was difficult to see in the dark. I was in the mountains. At about 12:00 midnight or so, I came to what I thought was a curve to the right in the highway. I was wrong. I suddenly confronted a "T" intersection. I slowed down, but I couldn't stop.

I went off the end of the highway and down into the ditch, but I somehow kept the bike up. I quickly got my Yamaha back on the road and looked both ways—not a car in sight. I pulled out and went left. I only made it a block before a patrolman pulled me over. He said, "Just stay there, I just want to make sure you are okay." I explained I was okay, but that I had thought the road curved and I didn't have the right kind of visor for these conditions. I didn't see the T intersection until too late.

I was done for the night. I asked him if he knew how far it was to a motel. He told me to stay on the road till I came to the next town. A place on the left had cabins. The officer instructed me to head to the main cabin and wake up the manager. As he was talking, I could hear the swiftly running water of the rapids in the river on the other side of the road. I was lucky.

I thanked the officer and kept moving. I found the cabin place and woke the manager. I got a cozy place with two bedrooms, a living room, and a kitchen for $12.00. I counted my blessings and thought of my buddies

I left to sleep on the shoulder of the cold and lonesome road.

The next day was the second of July. My birthday was the third, and I was determined to get home on my birthday. I set out early. I had a long way to go. I had to sit in line with cars in Denver as they were rationing gas. That just wasn't fair. I only needed a few gallons to top off, and I couldn't go more than one hundred twenty miles or so, but I waited twenty minutes at least and then went on my way.

Somewhere in western Nebraska, I stopped to top off again and I took all the gear off my bike to add oil to my Autolube injection tank. Then these two guys from California, who were riding bikes, one a Honda four cylinder inline (probably a 650 with a windjammer) and the other a beautiful chopped 750, came up to me and asked, "You got all that stuff on your bike?" They watched as I put my gear all back on when I was done fueling. They asked if they could ride with me, and I agreed. I was honored to be riding with such a beautiful metric chopper.

We were cruising eastward on I-80. I was running side-by-side with the chopper. So cool. We had a tail wind. The guy on the smaller bike with the Windjammer pulled up alongside us and set his cruise control. He reached in his fairing's glove box and pulled out a camera. I swear he threw a leg over the tank and rode sidesaddle and took pictures of us. Man, I would love to have one of those pictures. We stopped together for gas a couple of times, and I finally left them behind when they pulled off the freeway and headed home on a two-lane road.

Endgame—Mike

I was committed totally to getting home by my birthday. I kept riding, blasting through the night, and finally passed under the overpass to my home town, Aurora, right at midnight. I rode to the next exit where there was an all-night truck stop. Nearly famished by now, I treated myself to a steak and eggs breakfast for under five dollars. I called my grandparents to let them know I was having breakfast and would be home within the hour. I had done it. I estimated it to be seven hundred thirty-five miles in one day. Give or take a few, I didn't care. I had gone from the Colorado/Utah border all the way to eastern Nebraska in one day.

Colorado—Brian

I remember when we got into Colorado, the three of us were west of Grand Junction when it was getting dark. Jeff and I weren't motivated to do any death-march riding that day, so we went off the highway, where road construction was going on, and had some sort of Team Black Rock council. After quick goodbyes and all that, Mike got on his chopper and road off, heading eastward, into the night. We listened to his Yamaha moan heavily down the highway until the sound completely disappeared. Then Jeff and I threw our sleeping bags out on the ground and spent the night.

We got up the next morning and rode into Grand Junction and ate breakfast at a restaurant (not fast food). We rode through the beautiful, forested Colorado mountains. I remember, as we were approaching Denver, we were on I-70 and we were traveling eastbound down a long hill just east of Floyd Hill and my bike, in fourth gear, was rapping high RPMs. This was one place on the trip where I felt not having fifth gear was a hindrance. (I live in Colorado now. For some reason, every time I go down that same hill, even today, I remember riding on that Yamaha in fourth gear!)

In Denver, we stayed with my uncle and aunt, Bill and Shirley Franzen. My cousins Steve and Mark entertained us. Jeff and I and my cousins went up a hill after dark, where we could look south toward downtown Denver. It was a great cityscape view! My cousin Steve took us to a "3.2" bar up on Lookout Mountain. Colorado was a 3.2 state (alcohol content of beer) for eighteen-year-olds at the time. We had a few 3.2 beers during the evening, and when Steve drove home, in his short-wheel-base Oldsmobile, I intentionally went to sleep so as not to watch the spectacle of drunk driving down twisting mountain roads in the middle of the night.

Here is an interesting fact. We had a little party in Beatrice the night before we left on our trip two weeks earlier. And Jeff and I celebrated a little bit on Lookout Mountain, but that was all. We flourished on soft drinks, water, and ice tea the whole road trip otherwise. You might say the parties were "bookends" to an otherwise sober experience!

Heading east from Denver the next morning on I-76, we ran into some rain. I thought I remembered it to be the only rain we rode in the entire trip, but we did run into a little rain in Kansas earlier.

Mike's seven hundred thirty-five miles in one day is crazy. My best might have been six hundred miles.

On my Yamaha, I would set the trip meter and when I got to one hundred miles, I would stop for gas and to shake out the two-stroke vibration and stretch. I surely needed a stretch. Man, seven hundred thirty-five miles!

Endgame—Brian

At the end of the trip, back in Nebraska after two weeks of hard riding and great adventures, Jeff "dropped off" at Aurora to celebrate July 4th with his family, and I continued alone, eastward, the twenty or so miles to my home in York. I remember approaching town almost ceremoniously, thinking about the sense of being a "victor." There have been other times in my life, when I've backpacked in the wilderness for four days, or driven into new states, or paddled in Boundary Waters in Minnesota, and had that same sense of overcoming, as achieving a victory. I kind of expect people to celebrate my accomplishments with me but have come to understand that others have no idea of the accomplishment and that I, as the individual who did the deed, must relish the experience alone, by myself. And that is sufficient and that is what memories are built on.

Endgame—Jeff

The ride from Grand Junction to Denver to home seemed like forever to me. It was time to go home. Of course, Colorado is scenic. What state can offer more? The Eisenhower tunnel was an engineering marvel. We passed through it only a few months after the tunnel was dedicated in March 1973.

Eisenhower Tunnel (Courtesy CDOT)

Brian's relatives in Denver were very hospitable—and I had an interesting introduction to the Rocky Mountain night life up on *Look Out Mountain*. But I was so ready to go home. We droned down I-80 on July 4th like zombie homing pigeons.

I made it to Aurora in time for the 4th of July picnic at my grandparents' (Sam and Blanche Ross) home. Everyone was glad to see me, but the picnic was ON when I arrived, and the family was pretty much occupied with eating great food. Later that evening, we had fun with fireworks at Uncle Valta's place just down the street. He lived in a nice two-story house that had a great backyard and a hill perfect for setting off fireworks.

Before leaving Aurora at ten pm that night, I unstrapped my gear and put everything in my folks' car (they had come to Aurora for the July 4th celebration). I suppose I thought it would be an easier or more casual ride without the "luggage." I was very careful to make sure all the hooked straps were tight, though, and not flopping around since they no longer had baggage to keep in place. The bike seemed naked without all that stuff perched on the seat.

My mom told my dad to follow me home, down Highway 34, to our home in York, so she could see I made it okay. It's kind of funny, or ironic, that my folks followed me the last thirty minutes of my trip. By eleven pm, I was home in York safely sleeping. My faithful R5 was finally able to rest. But I remember thinking how strange it seemed to have nowhere to go the next day, July 5th.

IV

Afterword by Doyle Ross

My son, Jeff, has asked me to give readers some insight into the thoughts and worries, if any, about him and his teenage friends when they embarked on their long trip on Yamaha 350s. I believe to give you the true feelings of myself and Jeff's mother about this adventure, I need to give you some insight into our history with the world of motorcycles.

Let's start, not with me, but with my own father. Samuel E. Ross was born in 1902, so you can be assured he grew up alongside motorized vehicles. I have a picture of him on his Harley Davidson when he was a teenager. I have no idea how he acquired the bike, but I know it was a belt drive and probably of about 1913 or 1914 vintage. By the way, his helmet at that time consisted of turning his cap around backward. (So, I guess he was well ahead of his time as now it seems the all hats are worn that way.) Anyhow, he lived on a farm in Nebraska with his family. One of his duties was to ride up to the nearest town and purchase repair parts for their farm machinery when it was broken. He told me that on one of his trips he had that Harley "on the boil" when he hit a rut. The bike threw him off and he landed in plowed field with his mouth open. It took him a long time to clear the dirt from his mouth.

S.E. Ross on his 1914 Harley near Stockham, Nebraska

He was married in 1925, and I arrived on the scene in 1927. When I was two years old, I began my life long acquaintance with motorcycles. By this time in his life he had moved to his own farm with his bride and infant son. At the time, the only vehicle he had other than a tractor was a Harley sidecar outfit. My mother liked to tell about the time they had taken the sidecar rig to town to buy groceries. On the way home, there was a torrential rain storm, and she said the pair of us were almost washed out of the sidecar.

When I was sixteen years old, my dad bought “me” a used 1940 Harley 45-cubic inch motorcycle from a local farmer. I am sure he told my mother it was a gift for me. Dad and I spent a lot of happy hours just working on the bike and adding some accessories. I rode that bike many a mile over the gravel roads of central Nebraska.

My dad was a dealer for the Gleaner Baldwin Combine company at that time. He was also appointed as a dealer for the Allis Chalmers Co. We then moved to a larger town, Aurora, that had a railroad. In 1948, we secured dealership rights from the Indian Motorcycle Co. My younger brother, Valta, and I were a very happy couple of kids. However, this was about the time when Indian was in serious money trouble because of financial mismanagement by their executive team.

Doyle Ross on a Royal Enfield and his dad, S.E. Ross, on an Indian motorcycle circa 1950, Aurora, Nebraska.

In 1949, Indian began producing new lightweight vertical twin motorcycles. We sold one of the first ones to a friend of ours. This was an Indian Scout, a 26-cubic inch bike. I don't know who came up with the idea, but my brother, Valta, Chris, our friend who bought the Scout, and I decided it would be great fun to take a long trip on those bikes. Do you see the similarity between this adventure and the one my son is writing about? Life is certainly strange and wonderful.

We ordered two new Indian Scouts, one a bright yellow and one red. Chris had a green model. We began our discussions on when and where we would go. We finally decided to leave Nebraska, head south, and travel to New Orleans. Why? Well, it sounded right. Then we would cut across country to Ohio where several relatives of my mother resided. After a short stay, we would head west back to Nebraska. Remember now, the roads were two lanes, cell phones were unheard of, and road service was in your tool kit.

We got the idea to wear matching jackets. We bought the jackets, and a local lady embroidered the “The Unholy Three” on the back of each jacket. We were BAD. What about the best laid plans of...? It turned out one of the Unholy Three, Chris, could not make the trip. His mother would not let him go. Now we were the Unholy Two.

Now to add to our problems, about a week before our planned date to leave, a customer rode into our shop on a 1947 Harley. When he saw the Scout I was going to use on the trip, he decided to trade for that bike. So now the Unholy Two were riding a used Harley and new Indian on the adventure.

Finally, we left on our trip. I was a little apprehensive since I had ridden that Harley for only ten or twenty miles since the trade.

Our first minor mishap was in a small town in Kansas when a truck we were following decided to slam on his brakes. I also slammed, well, I applied the brakes on the Harley. It did not speed up, but it sure didn't slow down much, either. It slid out from under me and we both hit the asphalt. No damage to bike or rider except a small chrome strip was scraped off the Harley's fuel tank.

My brother is and was a real funny, comic guy. We were heading south and stopped at a roadside cafe for a burger. A local know-it-all sauntered over and threw a smirk and asked us what happened to the third member of the Unholy Three alliance. We were wearing those jackets I mentioned before. My brother stopped eating his burger long enough to casually remark that he was run over by a truck up in Kansas. Then he reached for another french fry, just as casually.

That was the last we heard from the local.

When we entered the city of New Orleans, we were riding in a cloudburst. It was raining so hard some of the autos had stopped because their windshield wipers would not take the water off. We were already soaked so we just motored on until Valta saw a vacancy sign.

We spent about three days there, then headed north east. Got to Ohio with no troubles and got acquainted with many of my Grandad's brothers. These family members were from my mother's side of the tree.

After a few days, we stomped on the kick starters and headed home. Got back in a few days, tired but with a lifetime of memories.

Both bikes ran great, although the old Harley did live up to its infamous reputation of those years' bikes. I thought that somewhere in Iowa it seemed to have lost some of its vibration. After a few days at home we did an examination to get it ready for sale and discovered a couple engine mounts had broken. Oh yes, the vibration was still there, but it just wasn't getting to the frame.

I know it was a great trip my brother and I made because some sixty years later, many of the details of the trip are still vivid in our minds. I am glad we rode down to New Orleans.

Valta and a 1951 Indian (Photo courtesy Valta Ross)

Valta and his Vincent Black Shadow (Photo courtesy Valta Ross)

So, this started out with a question concerning the parents' feelings about their son hitting the motorcycle trail. As for me, I really believe my father felt the same way I did some thirty years before. Not fear or worry but envy. My dad, I am sure, wished he could have had the opportunity to have an adventure like mine. For myself, Jeff's trip brought back memories of my own some twenty-five years before. I can't speak for my own mother's feelings about her two sons' trip, but I know she understood we were good riders and had common sense. I knew Jeff's mother had been on and around motorcycles all her married life, and she also knew Jeff was a good rider, the bikes were dependable and Jeff, like me, had a good helping of just plain old common sense.

Valta and Doyle Ross reminisce at Crosswinds Restaurant in Payson, Arizona, March 2019

V

Thoughts in 2019

Thoughts in 2019—Mike

Years after the trip, in the late seventies and eighties, I played my first team sport—softball. Several of the guys playing in the league had bikes. There were Yamaha Virago 750s, Kawasaki KZ650s, and Yamaha XS650s. For a while I rode a Suzuki GS425, and then later, a Kawasaki KZ650SR (a dandy bike that was dependable but buzzy on a long ride).

I was the pitcher for our softball team. And when I would hear the unmistakable sound of a Kawasaki triple or Yamaha twin while I was on the mound, I would simply stop the game and put my hand up to my ear and grin. Oh, I caught heck for it, but I didn't care. I loved the two-strokes, and everybody knew it.

What happened to my chopped 350? I traded that bike for a '63 Chevrolet Impala with a balanced 327, Hooker headers, four-speed SS. It was crazy fast, fun, and loud. Sold it. Bought the bike back and sold it again.

In 2004, I had just been fired from my job of thirty years. My company had closed the store after it had been sold out. I was lost. Then, coincidentally but also typically, our refrigerator went out, just quit working. My wife Pam and I went to the family-owned appliance store in Beatrice to pick out a new fridge. As we walked up to the front entrance, I noticed the motorcycles under the awning behind the fence of the shop next door. There it was. A Yamaha FZ1!

I had recently written Yamaha a letter asking them when they were going to bring the "Fizzie" to America. I knew they had released it the FZ1 earlier in Europe as a test market, and I also knew then I wanted one. Very badly.

I grabbed my wife by the arm and said, “See that bike over there? I’m buying that.” She said, “No, you’re not! You have three motorcycles in the garage now.” To which I simply replied, “You see that bike over there? I’m buying that.”

Mike, his FZ1, and his faithful dog Dexter

(Just a slight interjection by Jeff. Mike doesn’t say much about this, but he has become quite a motorcycle mechanic and vintage bike restorer. Check out a few of his successful restoration projects below.)

Yamaha XS 650 Café Racer

1985 Honda VFR 500

1981 Yamaha Seca 650

1979 Honda CX 500

Mike and the 1977 RD 400 Project

Well, Jeff is right. I have put a lot of time and effort into restoring "vintage" motorcycles. Here's the story of my '77 Yamaha RD 400. Actually, buying it was almost as interesting as restoring it!

Back in about 2007 or so, I found this Yamaha project bike on Craigslist. The Yamaha was said to be in original condition but with bent front forks. I didn't even notice the fork problem in the pictures.

The bike was in Omaha, Nebraska, about eighty-five miles from Beatrice where I live. It was late in the evening when I saw the for-sale notice, and I immediately called the owner and indicated I would purchase the bike at full asking price, $1000. I offered to make the two-hour drive to meet him, but I let him know I would have to pay by check since I didn't have that much cash on hand.

He agreed to wait until the next day to make the deal—with a condition. So, I could drive up after work the next day, but I had to bring cash. What worried me was that he insisted on cash. Not only that, but he wouldn't give me an address where I could pick up the bike. The owner insisted we meet at a gas station. He would then have me follow him to the exact location where I could pick up the bike.

Now this wasn't exactly a good neighborhood, and I was more than a little bit uneasy about going to an undisclosed location with a pocket full of cash.

But I wanted the bike THAT BAD!

So, I went. My wife went with me. My son was actually working in Omaha a few miles away from the scheduled buyer/seller rendezvous. We met up with my son, and then I had them follow me in a separate car. As we planned, I met the seller at the gas station. Then my wife and son discretely followed me.

Our cell phones were on speaker phone mode as we drove to the bike's location.

They had instructions to call 911 immediately if I gave them the signal. I didn't tell them I had a .357 revolver and my .40 Smith & Wesson within easy reach in case things went south.

But I was willing to take the risk. I wanted that bike. We drove to an apartment complex and, from the entrance, I could see several bikes that had been rolled out of a garage space to get to the back. There stood the RD400! I knew the deal was legit, so I give my family the-all clear sign to come on in.

The paper work was completed, and the money exchanged. We loaded up my "new" bike and headed out to celebrate our good fortune. The bike needed a lot. The parts list was getting longer the closer we looked, but I didn't care. It was mine!

I wanted to attach clip-ons (handlebars), but I went with drag bars for comfort. I replaced the bent front forks with straight ones I already had. I rebuilt the brakes and fitted new seals and stainless-steel brake lines. With patience, I rebuilt the carbs, put in new points and condensers, plugs, and I even put on a new seat cover.

Eventually, I sourced a vintage set of DG expansion chambers (exhausts). I modified the kick start to fit. I also installed a new chain and sprockets along with new tires.

Mike Installing DG Expansion Chambers on the lovely 1977 RD 400

I was most proud of the rearsets (racing-style foot pegs). I purchased a set of really nice RD350 rearsets and machined them to fit the RD400 seamlessly. You would never know they were originally designed for the RD350 model. My fitment was something I don't think has been done since and should probably be marketed.

The bike ran hard, handled, and was a blast to ride with a sound I will always love.

Later I sold the RD to Brad at HVC Cycles in Lincoln. He used the bike as a test-bed for new accessories and equipment. Turns out he blew up the engine on that thing during a tire burnout contest. But I heard he rebuilt it.

I think the RD now has the best of everything.

I regret letting that Yamaha go. I know my thinking at the time was: "It's now in the best condition it could possibly be with the resources I have. If I keep it and something happens to it, it will become a money pit or I might lose all my investment."

Jeff is always saying he wishes he would have kept all the bikes he rode earlier in life. Hah. We would probably need an empty grocery store or warehouse to hold all of our past machines!

V

Thoughts in 2019

Thoughts in 2019—Brian

On our 1973 trip, the road was what we were about—the next curve, the next hundred miles, what we would pass and see. Just being outside was magnificent. And we had great riding weather for almost the entire trip.

Everything was blocked out in one hundred-mile increments. In hindsight, that was a crazy-ass way to ride. No one would do it on a 350 two-stroke in 2019. We rode right to the ocean on those Yamahas and stuck our fingers and toes in the water...and loved the moment.

My wife and I took a fun cruise and sightseeing trip to Alaska in June 2018. Once ashore in Alaska, we rode a lot of buses, which were obviously driven by others. When sitting further back in a bus, a person only gets to see out the window and a little across the aisle. I noticed I never really saw where we were going.

Driving yourself gives the traveler the whole, the complete, experience, especially on a motorcycle. You get to see everything coming at you, probably in a two hundred seventy-degree arc. You experience the temperature changes, the smells, the rain, the cold, the heat. On a bus, a traveler gets moved from one discrete location to the next spot and, even if separated by eight hours, it feels like twenty miles. Driving yourself may be more tiring, but I believe it to be a superior experience. Is motorcycling the American West travel experience at its best? Surely!

Thoughts in 2019—Jeff

Jeff in June 2018 buying a new Kawasaki Ninja 400

In the *Bad Day at Black Rock* movie, Macreedy (Spencer Tracy) went to the small desert town of Black Rock looking for a man. I guess Team Black Rock headed across the desert to become men. Today, in 2018, I am still riding. My daily ride now is a 2018 Kawasaki EX400 Ninja. I also have a 2006 Kawasaki Bayou 250 quad, and a restored 1972 Yamaha CS3 200 two stoke (whose engine looks just like an R5's engine in miniature!).

Yamaha CS3 200 CC

My son has a 2013 Honda CBR 250R. (Yes, I have always enjoyed small displacement motorcycles.) Of course, my dream is that Quinten and I can someday ride together across the burning desert to the blue Pacific—or at least to Nebraska.

Quinten Ross on his CBR 250R

VI

Later Rides

Summer of 2014

60th Birthday Motorcycle Run—Brian

My boys and I have made it a tradition, for a number of years, of doing some recreation together around the first week of August, and they wanted to do something special for my 60th birthday. My youngest son, Adam, had just bought a KTM Adventure motorcycle and didn't want to keep two similar-purpose bikes, so he gave his Kawasaki KLR to me, as he knew riding had been a big part of my life. I spoke often of enjoying riding, but I hadn't ridden since before Adam was born. He wanted to give that bike to me. Aaron, my oldest, joined us, and we went on an Adventure Cycling ride into the mountains of central Colorado. We wanted to see how many mountain passes, paved or gravel, we could ride over in three days.

Starting the ride in front of my house in Aurora, CO

We left from my house in Aurora, CO around four pm. We knew we were riding into rush hour in Denver, so we took side streets to Quebec and C-470 where we got on that interstate highway and rode to the Morrison exit, where we turned west to Evergreen, for our first break. Adam remembers how aggressive I rode, but motorcycle riding is like knowing how to swim; the muscle memory is always there. We journeyed on to the Echo Lake Lodge at the entrance to the Mt. Evans highway, where we added additional layers to our coats and clothing. It had showered a little rain on the way up, causing the air to be chilly, plus it was getting close to dark.

We continued on Highway 103 to Idaho Springs where we jumped onto I-70. We rode through the Eisenhower-Johnson Tunnel, which marked our first mountain pass (riding through the tunnel, across the Continental Divide). Darkness had fallen, and we exited the freeway at Frisco. I took the lead here because the KLR was the slowest of the three cycles. As we left I-70, I remember on the exit we passed a deer with a full set of antlers in the ditch (where it thankfully stayed). We rode south on Highway 9 to Breckenridge, where we ate at a restaurant and stayed the night at the Breckenridge Hotel.

The next morning, we ate breakfast, gassed up the bikes, and headed south from Breckenridge. We took a quick left onto the Boreas Pass road. That road turned to gravel in a few miles. At the top of Boreas Pass, we noted the dilapidated railroad buildings and grade, which served the gold mining in the late nineteenth century at nearby Breckenridge. Aaron attached his GoPro camera to his helmet and recorded a good number of action riding photos.

Brian and Aaron in Buena Vista, CO

Heading down the south side of Boreas Pass, we got onto Highway 285 and turned west to Johnson Village and then north on Highway 24 to Buena Vista. We rested here and put gas in the motorcycles. We headed west from Buena Vista and soon crossed the beautiful wide vista of Cottonwood Pass with Taylor Park Reservoir just to the west of the pass. We continued on from the pass, with the Taylor River running right next to the road on the way down, to the junction at Highway 135. We turned north on the highway and rode into Crested Butte where we parked on Main Street and ate lunch at a restaurant, watching some soccer in the World Cup on the TV.

Riding on a gravel road west of Crested Butte, CO

After lunch, we headed west towards Kebler Pass. After about 10 miles, the road surface turned dusty gravel. After crossing the Pass, we descended to Highway 133, which took us north on a curvy highway, where we remember getting into a rhythm of riding hard on our bikes through the corners. We passed Marble and Redstone and ended the day in Carbondale. Adam knew the town well, as he resided here during a summer construction internship. We ate dinner at his recommended restaurant and stayed the night in Carbondale.

In the morning, we ate breakfast at the inn then suited up and turned east on Highway 82, heading towards Aspen. We rode through Aspen and headed up 82, through a lot of curves on the highway, which, again, were fun to take on motorcycles, heading towards Independence Pass. This was a brisk, beautiful blue-sky morning with some puffy white clouds. We stopped on the Pass for rest and took photos.

Heading down from Independence Pass, we drove past Twin Lakes on our right. We intersected with Highway 24 north of Buena Vista and rode into town. We tried to find lunch, but the place was so busy with tourists, we decided to head on. We turned east on Highway 285 and crossed Trout Creek Pass from the west, for the second crossing of that pass in two days. At Antero Junction, we turned east on Highway 24 and rode on to Woodland Park where we finally ate lunch.

From Aspen, riding up to Independence Pass

Brian (in the middle) standing up to stretch while approaching Independence Pass

Approaching Independence Pass

Approaching Independence Pass

The Franzen boys at the summit of Independence Pass

Adam and Brian

Ready to ride down from Independence Pass

Leaving Woodland Park, we turned north on Highway 67 for a nice paved mountain highway. At Deckers, which sits on the South Platte River, we turned east and rode along the river on a gravel road to Sedalia. We turned north, then on Highway 85, and rode home. The temperature rose into the nineties from the cool, comfortable mountain temps we had been riding in for two days, making the jackets seem too much.

We traveled over seven hundred miles in three days, and we crossed seven mountain passes on this tour. I rode the 2009 Kawasaki KLR 650 (bored out to 680cc), Adam rode his orange KTM 990 Adventure, and Aaron rode a Kawasaki 650 Versys he borrowed from Adam's friend, as Aaron flew into Denver from out-of-state. All the bikes performed flawlessly, and it was a beautiful ride on motorcycles together in the mountains. It was a great way to celebrate my 60th birthday, with a renewal of the summer fun outing with my boys.

Brian next to his KLR on Independence Pass

Bit of a Reunion Ride for Mike and Jeff—May 2019

From Nebraska to St. Johns, AZ—Mike

On May 26, I rode out of Beatrice on my Gen 1 2001 Yamaha F Z1000. I had hoped to be riding with a friend, but he had to have surgery, so he was unable to get on his motorcycle for several months. I was determined it was now or never for my ride to Arizona, and I went ahead with my plans. Since I was going solo, I decided to only spend one night on the road to save money. Motels aren't cheap anymore. I set an ambitious goal: To ride to Tucumcari New Mexico in one day. The distance was approximately 590 miles.

Nebraska had experienced a cool spring, and it was chilly that morning I left. I insisted on waiting to leave till the temperature was 70 degrees F. That's my comfort threshold for extended trips. I didn't want to screw things up by getting hypothermia right out of the gate, especially since I had a long way to go.

Word had spread around town that I was riding solo to Arizona thanks to my buddy, Ben Bird. Fortunately, on the day I set out, I was joined by three riders: Ben Bird, Sean Brooks, and Stoney Brooks. They were going to escort me for an hour to Washington, Kansas and then turn around. That made a nice morning ride for them, and we all felt better about me not starting out alone.

(I was a little concerned about my recent new chain install. The chain might fail in those first few miles. It was, after all, the first time I had done such a job with a rivet master link.)

When we first rode out of Beatrice, I noticed they planned on riding behind me. After about 30 miles, I pulled to the side of the road. We were just outside of Marysville Kansas.

I explained to them that I had the rest of the trip to “lead.” I encouraged them to go ahead and I would follow.

While we were stopped, a gentleman in a pickup passed us on the highway, turned around, and then got out to ask us if we needed any assistance. He explained he rode a motorcycle and was in the local American Legion Riders. I told him where I was headed, and I explained the other guys were giving me a sendoff. We thanked him for the offer of assistance, and then we continued on. How times have changed. That give me a good feeling since I was going to be on my own for a very long time.

The rest of the way to Washington KS, I got to watch the guys on their bikes and listen to their distinctive exhaust notes and the harmony they created. It was a good start to my trip. After they left and returned home, the bike was smooth and purred along. I eventually turned south. I went through Norton, Kansas and turned south at Philipsburg, went through Dodge City—and noticed there was a lot of standing water. I noticed the sky was clouding up. Plus, I had about a thirty-five mph cross wind all day. I gassed up in Liberal, Kansas, and then I got rained out. My luck ran out.

I got pretty wet. I had rain gear on and though it was sufficient, I should have had better rain gear. I just passed through Dalhart, Texas, checked my weather radar on the phone, and saw a long and narrow wall cloud on the radar page, but thought I could punch through it. But when I hit the cloud bank, the wind shifted from south to north and the ground was covered with hail. Instantly, I got the bike slowed down, pulled over, and put the "Fizzie" on its side stand. Even so, it was so windy, I had trouble holding on to my motorcycle so it wouldn't blow over. And I took some kind of shelter behind the bike on the road. The hail and wind were terrific. Hail was beating the right side of my body.

I probably stood there for ten or fifteen minutes, but it seemed like forever. I was wet and cold; water had found its way into my jacket and boots. Finally, the storm passed, and I headed to Tucumcari, New Mexico, where I had a motel reservation. I was still an hour away, but I had to go.

Of course, I made it and warmed up a little. I used a hair dryer to dry off clothes. Water came out of my helmet. I probably spent two hours drying clothes and possession. I changed clothes and went to get something to eat. I was really hungry because I hadn't eaten all day. I was afraid to leave my bike unattended at any restaurant or gas station.

I was now basically retracing the route Brian, Jeff, and I took back in 1973.

The next morning was the start of a more relaxed, shorter day. The change in landscape was quite obvious. I stopped at the Very Large Array on Highway 60, and a family took a picture of me. I learned they were from Finland. Later I crossed the Continental Divide, cooled off again, saw some elk, and eventually made my way to St. Johns, Arizona, where I met up with Jeff at his exotic Quonset hut cabin. I found it amazing that we met in windy Apache County, Arizona, on our motorcycles so many years later. I called him from Springville to tell him I was thirty to forty minutes away, and when I arrived, there he was! Crazy, but we were running propane heat at five pm in the afternoon. The day was cool and windy.

Mike at Very Large Array (radio telescopes) in New Mexico

At the Continental Divide in New Mexico

At Jeff's Big Steel Cottage in Arizona

Jeff and his Ninja 400 at Big Steel Cottage in St. Johns, AZ.

We ate some Mexican food at a local place in St. Johns. Jeff ran the propane furnace all night. The next morning, after the sun gained a little altitude and warmed the air somewhat, we headed back to Jeff's home place in Gilbert, Arizona. We rode through Snowflake, Heber, and Payson then eventually turned south to the Phoenix Metro area. The Rim Road, Highway 260, was amazing. The Arizona forest and meadows are lush and green.

Jeff's son, Quinten, met us about twenty miles north of Gilbert near the Saguaro Lake Marina. He rides a 2013 Honda CBR 250 R. We had a fun ride into town—did a little jog in the road and went over to Apache Junction to visit Jeff's parents.

Quinten and Mike with Superstition Mountain in the Distance

Mike, Quinten, and Jeff's parents Doyle and Pat Ross in Apache Junction, AZ.

I had a fun four days at Jeff's place—we went out to Queen Valley for some quad riding and shooting, visited motorcycle and archery shops, and spent quite a bit of time in his swimming pool cooling off. I fell in love with his dogs, Chef and Iris.

Mike on Quinten's Bayou 250 quad near Queen Valley, Arizona

Mike walking Iris and Chef in Gilbert, AZ.

I noticed the tires on my FZ1 were "cupping" a little bit—maybe an inflation issue—but overall, the bike ran just fine on my way down to Arizona.

Jeff

We had a great time with Mike. I enjoyed riding with him from St. Johns to Gilbert. Seeing him occasionally in my rear-view mirror—well, that brought back many memories. Funny how riding behaviors stay the same after forty-five years or so.

My Ninja 400 easily runs sixty-five to seventy-five mph, so I was able to maintain highway speeds without issue. I was very pleased with the performance of my "small" motorcycle on this four hundred thirty-mile overnighter, I have to tell you, these modern small four-stroke twins are very similar in performance to our old "smoky" 350s—quick accelerating and fun to ride! I believe the Ninja 400 will do a mid-thirteen quarter mile and top out at about one hundred twenty mph.

While Mike was in Gilbert, we went quad riding and trap shooting. We spent quite a few hours lounging in my swimming pool. The weather was very good here, with temps only in the mid-nineties. Of course, we cleaned and worked on our motorcycles and spent hours discussing the old days. I took the big FZ1 for a spin to see if I could detect any tracking issues (that tire problem mentioned above), but things seemed fine to me. Q and I rode with him as far as Superior, Arizona on our old friend, Highway 60, when he headed back to Nebraska June 1st. We had a great breakfast at Los Hermanos.

Mike and Jeff at Los Hermanos, Superior Arizona, June 1, 2019.

Mike leaving Superior, heading back to Nebraska, the morning of June 1, 2019.

Heading home to Nebraska from Gilbert, AZ—Mike

After walking Chef and Iris the dogs and saying my goodbyes to my furry friends, I left Gilbert on a warm Saturday morning. Jeff and Quinten rode along the first thirty-five miles to get me started on the right trail home. We headed up to higher ground—about 2500 feet elevation but still desert. We went to a nice café up in the hills and had a great breakfast. After we said our goodbyes, I took off. I wished they could have ridden further with me, because the next stretch of road was amazing. Beautiful canyons and nice sweeping curves. I was enjoying the ride. I knew I had a long way to go, so I kept my speed up when I could. I had to stay focused.

I was heading for Interstate 40 to set a fast pace home. I was making good time on I-40 when I came to one of many construction zones. Traffic was heavy with a lot of semis and motor homes. There was one particular stretch I found exceedingly annoying. The slow-down lasted maybe fifteen miles by the time everyone merged to one lane and got through. Speed was down to a crawl. Traffic was so slow, I couldn't even run first gear. I had to start and stop constantly. I frequently had to slip the clutch and walk the bike. The scenario was horrible. I had semis spewing fumes, the air was hot, and I was getting sick to my stomach. I was also afraid I was going to break my clutch cable, burn out the clutch, or overheat the motor.

After more than an hour of this, I started thinking about running out of gas before I could reach the next filling station. That was a constant issue. Especially when you are traveling by yourself. That worry would haunt me the whole trip. After an eternity, I left the construction zone and increased my speed, just like everyone else, hoping to finally get going. I pushed hard all day, just stopping for gas. I never went too far on a tank because I needed to get off and stand and stretch anyway, so I thought I might as well top off the fuel tank and ease my concerns.

Later in the day, I noticed I was getting seriously behind on my schedule. Daylight was beginning to fade. I still had a long way to go to get to Tucumcari. I stopped for gas again, and I called the motel and told them I would be late but I would make it. I checked the radar on my phone as I noticed lightning and threatening clouds in the direction I was heading. Sure enough, there was a storm heading the same direction, and it was already raining in front of me. Another smaller rain shower was sweeping in behind. I decided to get something to eat and give the storm a chance to move ahead. After a burger, I set out. I got behind a semi and used his lights to see further up the road. Rain had just passed, so I was getting hit with the spray. I decided to just lie down and become part of the bike. I tucked in and stayed with my semi as best as traffic allowed My plan worked and I made it to Tucumcari!

The next morning, I got a decent start. I knew I had to push myself to get home. One good thing was the sky was clear. I hadn't gone far when I passed a motor home I had passed several times before yesterday, so I gave them a wave as I went by. About an hour into the ride, I noticed something crossing the highway in front of me. At first, I thought it might be a rabbit, but it was black and moved differently. When I got close, I saw it was a tarantula! Holy smokes, that thing was big. I barely missed the creature, and the big spider gave me the willies. I was glad to put that behind me.

I was using my phone to navigate since my GPS wasn't working. I plugged in my home address went with it. New Mexico flew by. So did Texas and Oklahoma. Kansas was another story. The Jayhawker state seemed to go on forever. Of course, I was going east and north, so it would be a lengthy ride.

Unexpectedly, things started to unravel a bit. I was on a highway that was not on the lousy map I had for back up. Neither were the towns. My old-time paper map was of the United States, so it didn't have a lot of detail. Then the worry began about the gas stops again. I kept stopping to try to figure out where I was, but nothing was familiar.

Finally, I pulled into a gas station and a couple pulled up in a car with Nebraska Custer County license plates. When they got out of their car, I asked if they knew my friend Shawn Harvey. They DID! Small world. With a promise to tell him "Hi" for me, they pulled out of the station, and I continued. I realized the route I was on was taking me to Salina, Kansas. I was making good time. I finally became more confident of the distance I could go with each tank of gas, but I was becoming physically sore. It was hard to stay on the bike, so I stopped and added a sheepskin seat cover (I was carrying it in a bag) for comfort. The seat cover helped some, but I was beyond too far gone. Those last miles were painful.

Once I arrived straight south of York, Nebraska on Highway 81, I absolutely knew where I was. I bought gas one more time in Concordia and made the final push. I did the math and knew I could make it. Next stop was home. I had phoned ahead and told Pam I thought I would be home around 8:00 pm. I was home almost exactly as promised. Pam was waiting on the porch to welcome me.

Mike and Pam Newlun moments after Mike arrived home in Beatrice Nebraska June 2, 2019.

It was good to be home safely after a **2375-mile round-trip**! Most of it was five hundred fifty plus miles at a time. Long days to be sure. My mind had been racing with all the things that could go wrong, but nothing happened.

I had to do one more thing as soon as I unloaded the bike.

I said thanks. Thanks to God for watching over me as I traveled alone.

But I wasn't really alone. It had been a wonderful, long-overdue reunion. Long overdue. I finally got to ride again alongside my buddy, Jeff. I have seen him many times since 1973, but we had never ridden together like in the old days. It just wasn't the same since we didn't get to ride together any more. This trip changed all that. My ride was redemptive for both of us.

Appendix

Top 50 Hits of 1973/Top 50 Songs of 1973
(Courtesy www.musicoutfitters.com)

Billboard Year-End Hot 50 chart for 1973.

1. Tie a Yellow Ribbon Round the Ole Oak Tree - Tony Orlando and Dawn
2. Bad, Bad Leroy Brown - Jim Croce
3. Killing Me Softly with His Song - Roberta Flack
4. Let's Get It On - Marvin Gaye
5. My Love - Paul McCartney and Wings
6. Why Me - Kris Kristofferson
7. Crocodile Rock - Elton John
8. Will It Go Round in Circles - Billy Preston
9. You're So Vain - Carly Simon
10. Touch Me in the Morning - Diana Ross
11. The Night the Lights Went Out in Georgia - Vicki Lawrence
12. Playground in My Mind - Clint Holmes
13. Brother Louie - Stories
14. Delta Dawn - Helen Reddy
15. Me and Mrs. Jones - Billy Paul
16. Frankenstein - The Edgar Winter Group
17. Drift Away - Dobie Gray
18. Little Willy - Sweet
19. You Are the Sunshine of My Life - Stevie Wonder
20. Half-Breed - Cher
21. That Lady, Pts. 1 & 2 - The Isley Brothers
22. Pillow Talk - Sylvia
23. We're an American Band - Grand Funk Railroad
24. Right Place, Wrong Time - Dr. John

25. Wildflower - Skylark
26. Superstition - Stevie Wonder
27. Loves Me Like a Rock - Paul Simon
28. The Morning After - Maureen McGovern
29. Rocky Mountain High - John Denver
30. Stuck in the Middle with You - Stealers Wheel
31. Shambala - Three Dog Night
32. Love Train - The O'Jays
33. I'm Gonna Love You Just a Little More, Baby - Barry White
34. Say, Has Anybody Seen My Sweet Gypsy Rose - Tony Orlando and Dawn
35. Keep On Truckin', Pt. 1 - Eddie Kendricks
36. Dancing in the Moonlight - King Harvest
37. Danny's Song - Anne Murray
38. Monster Mash - Bobby "Boris" Pickett & The Crypt Kickers
39. Natural High - Bloodstone
40. Diamond Girl - Seals and Crofts
41. Long Train Running - The Doobie Brothers
42. Give Me Love (Give Me Peace On Earth) - George Harrison
43. If You Want Me to Stay - Sly and The Family Stone
44. Daddy's Home - Jermaine Jackson
45. Neither One of Us (Wants to Be the First to Say Goodbye) - Gladys Knight and The Pips
46. I'm Doin' Fine Now - New York City
47. Could It Be I'm Falling In Love - The Spinners
48. Daniel - Elton John
49. Midnight Train to Georgia - Gladys Knight and The Pips
50. Smoke on the Water - Deep Purple

Glossary

Autolube: A mechanism on a machine for automatically lubricating a chain, engine, or other part. (Courtesy *Oxforddictionaries.com*) (Specifically, Yamaha's application and brand in text above)

BHP: BHP is the measurement of an engine's power without any power losses, while HP is BHP less the power losses. 3. HP is measured by hooking up the engine to a dynamometer, while BHP is measured in a controlled environment without anything attached to the engine (Courtesy *Differencebetween.net*)

Points and condenser ignition: The contact point ignition system consists of:

A battery or magneto to supply low voltage current for the spark
Mechanical contact points to control the point of ignition
A rotating cam to operate the contact points
A condenser to reduce arcing across the contact point surfaces
An ignition coil
A spark plug (courtesy *Thoughtco.com*)

Two-stroke engines: Noting or pertaining to an internal-combustion engine in which two strokes are required to complete a cycle (two-stroke cycle) one to admit and compress air or an air-fuel mixture and one to ignite fuel, do work, and scavenge the cylinder. (courtesy *Dictionary.com*)

Made in the USA
Monee, IL
24 November 2019

17365084R00071